Greeting Cards
from A to Z

JEANETTE ROBERTSON

Photos by Michael Hnatov

Sterling Publishing Co., Inc.
New York

DEDICATION

To Aunt Edith, Uncle Roy,
Grandma Rose, and Mother Viola
for nurturing my creativity

ABOUT THE AUTHOR AND ARTIST

Author and artist Jeanette Robertson began making handmade cards even before she went to grade school. She earned an Associate's Degree in Textile Design at the Fashion Institute of Technology and designed fabric patterns for various New York textile companies. Later she began selling her watercolor art to major greeting card companies.

Her love of patterns is evident in her handmade cards. "The use of pattern with texture and color is more fun than a challenge," Ms. Robertson says. She enjoys playing with the seemingly infinite combination of possible patterns and works toward inventing fresh new designs.

Ms. Robertson lives in Upstate New York with her husband Norman and their golden retriever.

Edited by *Jeanette Green*
Designed by *Rose Sheifer Graphic Productions*
Photos by *Michael Hnatov Photography*

Library of Congress Cataloging-in-Publication Data
Robertson, Jeanette, 1950 Oct. 15–
    Greeting cards from A to Z / Jeanette Robertson ; photos by Michael Hnatov.
        p. cm.
    Includes index.
    ISBN-13: 978-1-4027-2351-3
    ISBN-10: 1-4027-2351-2
  1. Greeting cards.   I. Title.
    TT872.R63 2006
    745.594'1—dc22

2 4 6 8 10 9 7 5 3 1

Published by Sterling Publishing Co., Inc.
387 Park Avenue South, New York, NY 10016
© 2006 by Jeanette Robertson
Distributed in Canada by Sterling Publishing
^c/o Canadian Manda Group, 165 Dufferin Street
Toronto, Ontario, Canada M6K 3H6
Distributed in the United Kingdom by GMC Distribution Services,
Castle Place, 166 High Street, Lewes, East Sussex, England BN7 1XU
Distributed in Australia by Capricorn Link (Australia) Pty. Ltd.
P.O. Box 704, Windsor, NSW 2756, Australia

Printed in China
All rights reserved

Sterling ISBN-13: 978-1-4027-2351-3
        ISBN-10: 1-4027-2351-2

For information about custom editions, special sales, premium and corporate purchases, please contact Sterling Special Sales Department at 800-805-5489 or specialsales@sterlingpub.com.

Contents

Introduction

In an age of fast food, fast cars, speedy computers, and impromptu e-mails, it's nice to sit down to carefully create a handmade card for a friend, colleague, aunt, sweetheart, child, parent, or someone dear. Making a handmade card shows how much you care. What says "I've been thinking about you" more than something crafted by your own hands and heart?

But not all card creations require slow time or artistic wizardry. In the few minutes it takes to fire up your computer, you can fashion a simple one-of-a-kind card.

The card-making techniques in this book range from the inexpensive (just use recycled materials found around your home) to the extravagant and can even include little gifts like baubles and beads. Whether you're a first-time or a seasoned card crafter, you'll discover fresh techniques that will inspire you to make up a card that's just right for the receiver. We've organized them from A to Z.

After you've chosen a particular technique and studied the finished cards, check the supply list before you begin. Be sure that you have all the necessary materials so that you don't have to stop midway and dash out to the store or a neighbor's house to find just what you're looking for.

We've included tags to identify "quick and easy" card-making techniques as well as other hints. We've also designed cards in a variety of styles. Since you'll have complete control of the creative process, you'll be able to define the style and finished appearance of the card. Depending on the materials you choose and how you put the card together, you'll be able to create cards that are elegant or simple, playful or serious, frilly feminine or handsomely masculine. It's up to you. Our examples are only intended to inspire you.

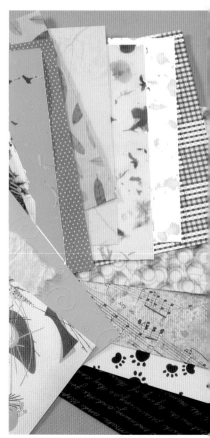

To make these cards uniquely your own, you could create your own rubber stamps rather than going out to buy them. Rubber stamps would allow you to make multiple cards that look a little alike or that have your personal signature, as it were.

Most of the A-to-Z techniques here allow you to decide how big or small you want the card and decorative elements. For selected cards, when you might need a little more guidance or when dimensions could influence design, we give measurements. If you keep a few standard envelope measurements in mind, that may help if you intend to mail the card. Otherwise, you can craft your own envelope. We'll show you how. Do keep in mind that the post office may charge more for square or unusual sizes of cards, so be sure to ask them or add extra postage if necessary. We advise that you mail the more delicate cards in padded envelopes for extra protection.

Card-Making & Card-Giving Hints

MATCHING CARD DESIGNS WITH RECEIVERS

If you want a handmade artsy card, create broccoli, potato, or onion prints; use snippets of various colors of tissue paper, decorative paper, or calligraphy to create a paper quilt. If you want to remember the 1960s, try a tie-dyed card. If you want to commemorate anniversaries, try framed cards or accordion photo displays. If you'd like to express a little wildness, try an outrageous card with oddities collected from around the house, wild animal stripes or spots, silly feathers, postage stamps, and cockeyed papers. For a formal appearance, use foil or vellum, make a black-and-white card, or use calligraphy or fancy computer-font initials.

For masculine cards, try wood texture; strong, dark colors; sporty objects, images, and decals; favorite photos; conservative stripes; necktie, fish, or car shapes; elements from nature, like bark and twigs; tag-shaped cards; wire or metallic embellishments; zigzag photo cuts; raffia; or squeegee prints.

For feminine-looking cards, try lace; doilies; cutouts; Victorian styles; silk flowers; ribbons; tissue, delicate, and flowery inclusion papers; filigree; baroque styles; and pastels.

For teenage girls, try shaped cards like flip-flops or a glittery telephone, rhinestone cards with personal initials (usually just the first name here), foam appliqués, silk flowers, favorite photos, pet themes, accordion folds, eraser-stamped cards and envelopes (invite teens to help you make them), hangings, inexpensive jewelry, lace, and tissue paper.

For teenage boys, try textures like wood or wool, magnets, sporty images, window cards, favorite photos, and computer-aided graphic designs.

For kids, try shaped cards, like teddy bears; textured cards, like our woolly creature; three-dimensional cards with foam appliqués or raised standout elements; kid die-cuts, alphabets, windows, and cutouts; or over-sized cards.

For those with limited vision, try oversized cards or cards with texture. Be sure to make the greeting grand and easy to read. Also work on contrasting colors so that any image or message can be easily seen.

The elderly may appreciate more traditional cards, but you probably know what your great aunt or grandfather likes. Keep in mind that the reading glasses are likely to come out when they sit down to look at your card. Mostly they'll appreciate (young tykes might not) the effort you took in creating something personal, just for them.

For free-form fun, try splatter, squeegee, or sponge prints. When you're in a hurry, make quick-and-easy cards by adding stickers, decals, or appliqués. Or recycle parts from old cards into a new one. A snip here and

there with deckle scissors can also create a fast but pleasing effect. Die-cut cutouts also can dress up an otherwise simple card.

For crafters, try yarn, quilt pins, quilted cards, button adornments, and colorful printed fabrics as well as felts, linens, and woolly and silky textures. Don't forget that brown paper bags make good, natural recycled material, whether for envelopes or elements of card décor. Ordinary tags (the kind used for prices and all sorts of things) can also become crafty-looking design elements.

For a challenge, try silhouettes, scherenschnitte, or paper quilling.

Cards that are their own gifts can include jewelry (small charm, ring, bracelet, or necklace); colorful paper clips; a lottery card inside a pocket; framed photos; a hanging, like a suncatcher or "stained-glass" window; kids' artwork; refrigerator magnets; bookmarks; or a gift pack of greeting cards.

Sympathy card designs best express elegant simplicity and dignity. Include the words "In Sympathy" or write your own heartfelt message. Embossed cardstock; vellum or linen papers; floral, tree, or leafy images; subdued designs; and pastels, whites, creams, and lavenders work nicely here. Avoid busy designs.

To make multiple cards, consider screen prints, vegetable prints, color photocopies of finished cards, printouts of computer-aided designs, silhouettes, ready-made cardstock with embossed designs, or using templates, patterns, or stencils. You could also make large sheets of paper with bubble-wrap, squeegee, splatter, salt, or sponge prints and cut the handmade printed paper into smaller cards.

Don't forget to fashion your own envelope, too. Make border designs with an eraser-stamp, use die-cuts and insert a contrasting colored paper underneath, try linings that coordinate with the card, cut flaps with deckle scissors, or write the receiver's name in calligraphy.

CARD-GIVING HOLIDAYS & OCCASIONS

You know all the usual card-giving holidays—Christmas, Valentine's Day, Mother's Day, Father's Day, Easter, Halloween, Thanksgiving, New Year's, St. Patrick's Day, Kwanza, Passover, and Chanukah—as well as the every-day-card occasions—birthdays, anniversaries, get-wells, friendship, sympathy, graduations, bar mitzvahs. And you've sent or received invitations and announcements for new babies and weddings, enclosed gift cards and tags, or written thank-you cards.

Around the world, festivals celebrate frogs and fish; the moon; animals; kites; snow; tiny paper boats floating with candles or sidewalk luminaria; and more. Imagine how delightful they could be for card-making. Why not April Fool's Day with its pranks and May Day with its rites of spring?

Just for fun, make up your own celebrations. Did your friend buy a new car? Make a card with car decals and a road map. To celebrate Aunt Edith's new puppy, make a card out of some stickers and include a gift certificate for dog food. Your friend began her own catering business, so wish her good luck with a card covered with food stickers, doilies, and miniature forks and spoons. Aunt Polly has just won a prize for her roses; congratulate her with a card featuring tiny silk roses tied with blue ribbon.

Get funky and send out cards for purple hair, pierced ears, a nose job, got a new boyfriend, your son's hard-rock band, got a dent in my car and my husband didn't kill me, Sherie and Avis made sandcastles at the beach, six-year-old Roy just baked his first cake, three-year-old Evan swallowed a button. You get the idea.

Naturally, you won't neglect tried-and-true announcements: Nicki moved into her new house, Toloa won a horse contest, Barbara's dog won the best-behavior award, Ellen took first place in a craft show, Susan finally sold that antique buggy, Kara has graduated from college, we retired and moved South, Kate is getting married, our folks celebrated their 50th wedding anniversary, Geryle has a new job, and more. To acknowledge such occasions, you could fashion, for instance, a house-shaped card, a gold medallion with a ribbon, embossed announcement, dog prints, a mortar made from black felt, images in gold foil, newspaper clippings of job ads arranged with colored-paper clippings, or a photo of your grandparents in a handmade frame card.

Since you'll be able to fashion quick cards yourself, you can honor selected friends when the appropriate month, week, or day arrives. Here are just a few: Black History Month (February), Women's History Month (March), Read-a-Book Month (December), National Firefighters' Week (week when September 11 falls; Canada), Nurse's Week (May 6–12), Administrative Professionals' Day (Wednesday of last full week in April), National Teachers' Day (Tuesday of first full week of May), or Grandparents' Day (first Sunday after Labor Day). Earth Day (April 22 or celebrated on the vernal equinox) and Arbor Day (varies by country and region) are celebrated across the globe.

Don't forget to write on the back of the card that it was hand-crafted by you. How could Sherie, Avis, Aunt Edith, and Norman resist loving you all the more?

You'll find some sources we've used on p. 160.

Accordion Folds

ACCORDION CARD PHOTO GALLERY

keepsake

Create a keepsake accordion photo gallery of your favorite pets or people. These make nice Christmas, anniversary, birthday, graduation, and family reunion gifts.

Here I use a sheet of 11 × 17-inch cardstock and cut it in half lengthwise. In Europe and other countries, long cardstock may vary from these measurements. Make adjustments accordingly. If you have long scrap paper, it's nice to first test your accordion size(s) before using good cardstock.

MATERIALS

extra long cardstock base (11 × 17 inch or about 28 × 43 cm)

paper cutter or sharp scissors

decorative paper

deckle scissors

two-sided tape

text

photographs (pets, family, or friends)

- Cut a long cardstock base in half lengthwise. For best results and a clean cut, use a paper cutter. The finished measurement will be about 5$\frac{1}{2}$ inches (14 cm) wide and about 17 inches (43 cm) long.

- Fold this cardstock accordion style. Four faces each about 4$\frac{1}{2}$ inch (10.8 cm) wide work pretty well. To achieve clean folds, you can score the cardstock.

- Use a decorative paper, with a theme if you wish, on the front of the card. For this project, I chose pet paw tracks.

- Inside the card are decorative holiday papers forming a simple frame for the photos you plan to mount. Cut all papers with deckle scissors slightly smaller than the four new card faces between the folds.

- Tape the decorative papers to the card with two-sided tape.

- On top of the decorative paper, tape the photos with two-sided tape.

- On small deckle-cut strips of paper, add the names of the pets or people. Or create these names with a computer printout on nice paper and then cut the names into small deckle-edge strips or nameplates. With two-sided tape, center the names below the pets or folks pictured.

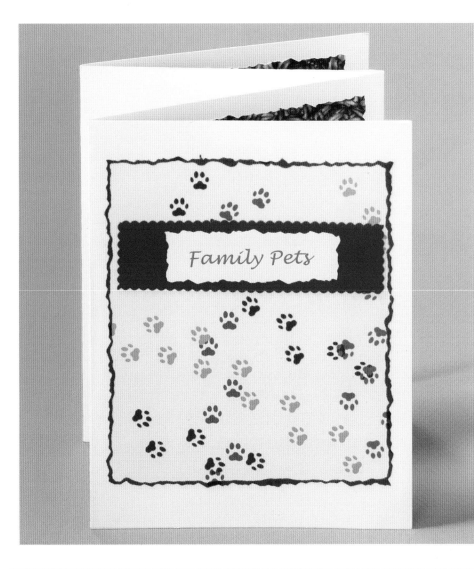

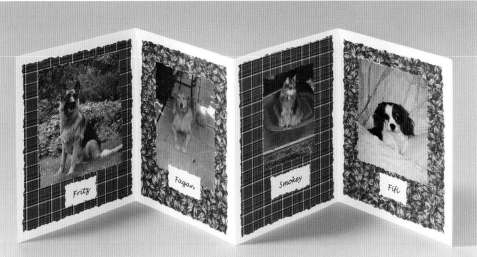

ACCORDION-FOLD INSERTS
challenging

Cards with accordion-folded inserts are multidimensional; the result is impressive. The recipient usually won't expect the surprise that's inside.

This card has assorted sizes and designs of hole-punch cutouts. It's made for a votive candle to sit in its glass container inside the open card. When the candle is lit, you'll see an array of dancing dots. Avoid fire hazards; do not leave the room when the candle is burning.

MATERIALS

ruler	long cardstock
pencil	legal-size paper for insert
craft knife	text
glue stick or two-sided tape	scoring tool
cutting mat	hole punches (assorted)

- To make the accordion-folded paper insert, use legal-size paper. Cut the paper to measure 5 x 12 inches (12.5 x 30.35 cm).

- For this to work correctly, you'll need an even number of folds; we use six folds here.

- Place the paper on a cutting mat. With a ruler and a pencil, measure and mark every 2 inches (5 cm) at both the top and bottom of the 5-inch (12.5-cm) sides. Then use the ruler and a scoring tool to carefully score the areas marked.

- Fold along the scores in and out to create zigzags (viewed from the edge) or an accordion.

Accordion folds for insert.

Firmly holding accordion-fold insert.

Bulldog clip holding accordion fold insert with punched decorative holes.

- Holding the assembly firmly with one hand, cut holes in horizontal rows with different sizes of hole punches. For design variations, you can make the "rows" wavy.

- After you complete punching holes in the entire length of the assembly, you can open the folded paper.

- Cut cardstock to 5 x 10 inches (12.5 x 30 cm). Score the center-fold area and fold. The card will be 5 x 5 inches (12.5 x 12.5 cm).

- You're now ready to attach the accordion insert to the card. Position the folds so that the accordion is inside the card. Make sure to fold the first and last section of the accordion in such a way that the backs of these sections face the inside of the card. Apply glue with a glue stick on one inside fold of the accordion.

- Carefully slip the first fold onto the cover and press the fold so that it adheres to the front edge of the cardstock. Repeat this process for the back of the card. (See photos of finished card.)

HINT: Test the fold position by simply sliding the accordion insert over the card before applying glue. Using ready-made text or text you have created on your computer or by hand on colored paper, you can glue the cutout text to the cover of the card.

IDEAS: Cut musical notes into the accordion for a musician, stars for an astronomy buff, flowers for the gardener, letters for a teacher, or frogs for that princess. Use stickers.

VARIATIONS

For fun variations, consider these ideas. Make a deeper accordion, include lots of designs and fun items, follow a theme, or use a paper print. Follow the directions above and instead of cutting holes, glue on photos, stickers, text, decorative paper scraps, or whatever you like. With a longer accordion insert, you can make more folded panels; just be sure to use even numbers of panels (and an odd number of folds). Attach decorative paper to the cover with a glue stick.

   After you finish decorating your accordion, follow the same directions above for attaching the accordion to the card. If you place a bulky item over a fold, you may need to rescore.

Alphabet
quick and easy

The alphabet can serve as decoration or the theme of a card. Here the letters themselves, whether from a typewriter, computer, handwritten script, or elegant calligraphy, become the focus. You can choose letters that are significant or simply spell out a message.

A quick-craft method is to use brads attached to the front of the card. We've found some here with letters that happen to match our sort of typewriter-key print background paper. We've added deckle-cut papers to fill it out.

MATERIALS

cardstock base or stiff decorative paper

colored or decorative paper

two-sided tape

deckle scissors

brads

one-sided tape

- Begin with cardstock or a stiff decorative paper. If your cardstock is plain, cut out decorative paper and attach it to the cardstock with two-sided tape.

- Cut strips from colored or decorative paper into ragged strips with deckle scissors.

- Secure the open brads on the back side of the "cover" cardstock with one-sided tape or package tape. So that the card looks good inside and to secure the brads, cover your work with another decorative or solid-colored paper lining on the verso side of the card face. Adhere the decorative paper to the cardstock with two-sided tape.

- Mail the finished card in a padded envelope.

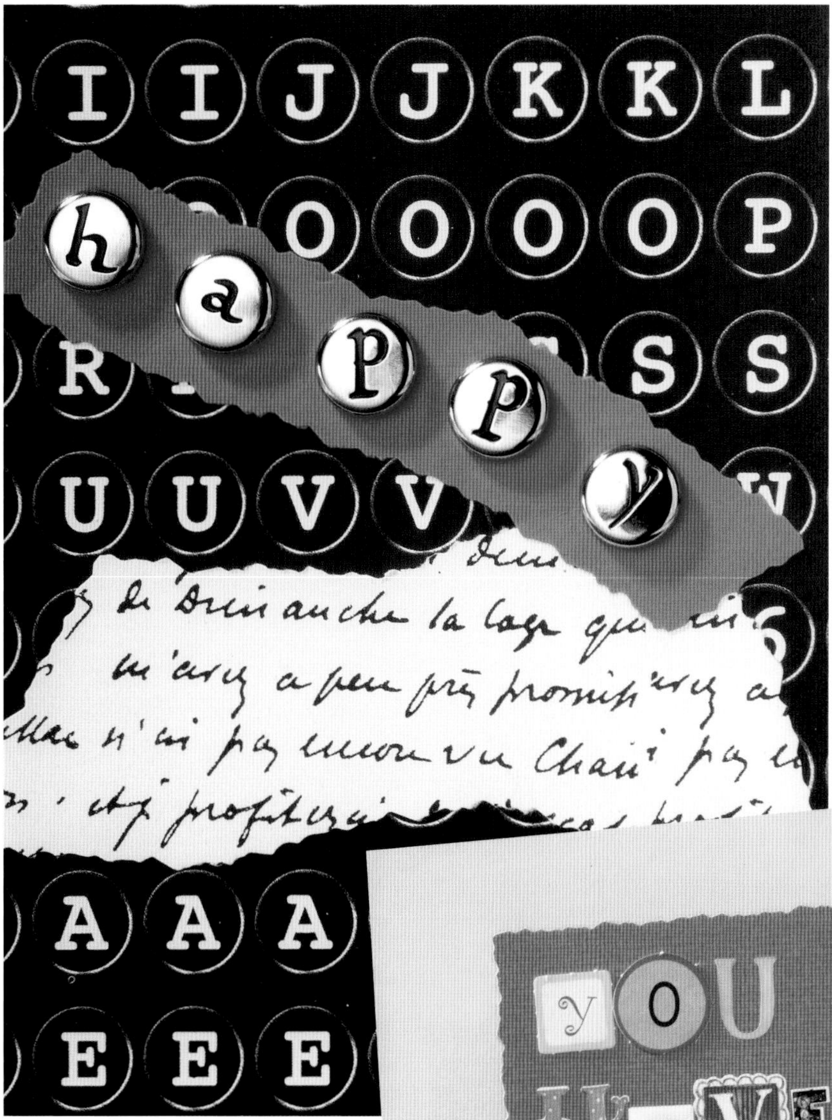
happy

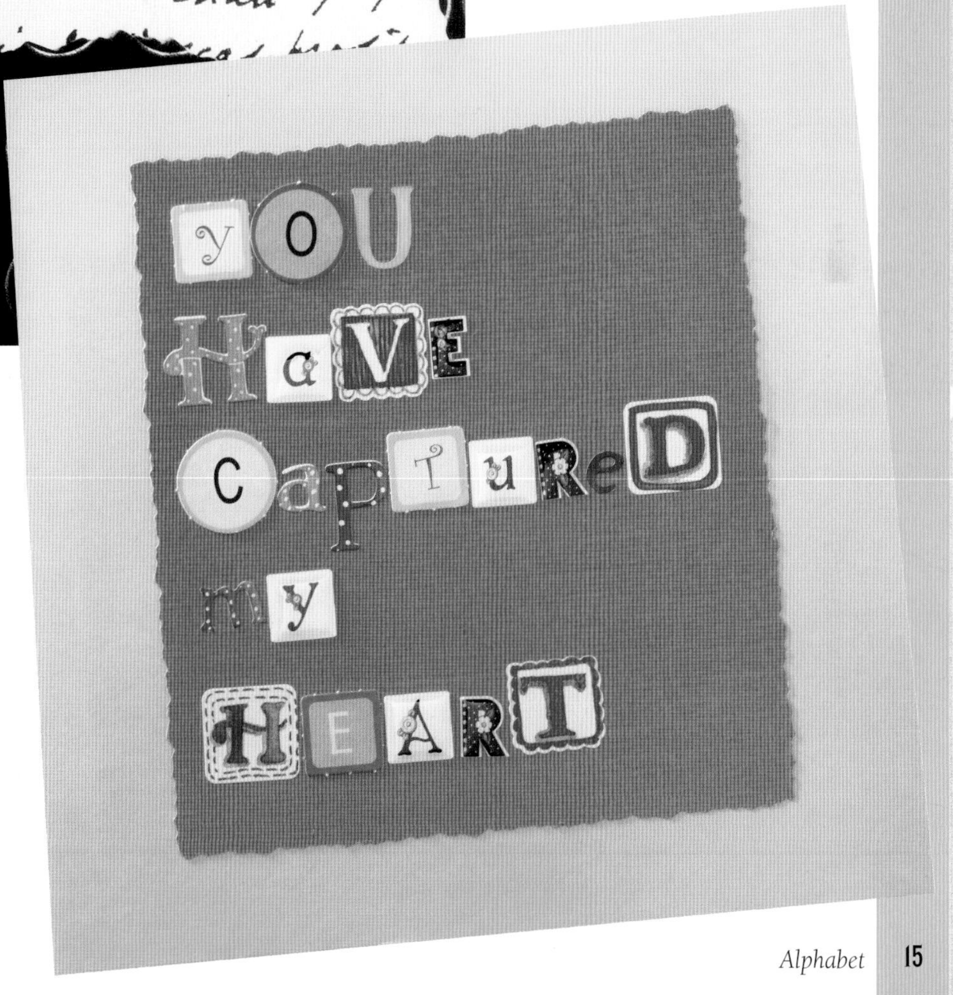
YOU
HAVE
CAPTURED
MY
HEART

Appliqués

quick and easy

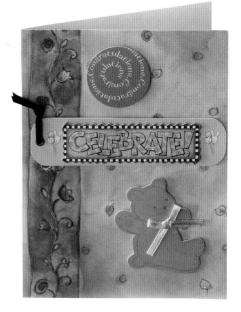

If you find yourself in a pinch for a last-minute card, you can create a quick card with just cardstock and appliqués.

Oops, you forgot that birthday or you wanted something to go with that gift you bought months ago for the cousin you'll be visiting tomorrow. Driving to a store can be inconvenient or take up precious time. Keep a supply of appliqués in your craft supply box. With a nice cache of appliqués, you'll be able to instantly craft a card to fit the many occasions that may arise.

MATERIALS

cardstock base
decorative paper
appliqué
two-sided tape
deckle scissors
optional embellishments

- Use ready-made cardstock base or cut your own cardstock.

- With deckle scissors, cut a decorative paper so that it's slightly smaller than the cardstock dimension. Adhere the decorative paper to the cardstock with two-sided tape.

- Again use two-sided tape to adhere the appliqué or appliqués to the decorative paper. If the appliqué comes with an adhesive backing, you will not need to add tape.

- If you have an appliqué message like "Congratulations," also add that to the decorative paper with its own adhesive backing or two-sided tape. As you wish, you can create your own banner message or simply write it inside the card. Or use brads.

- Mail finished cards in a padded envelope, as necessary.

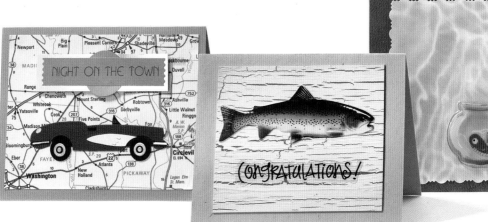

Booklet Cards

easy • multiple uses

Booklet cards work nicely for photos or vacation shots or mini-journals.

MATERIALS

cardstock base

decorative paper

deckle scissors

paper (with or without lines)

paper cutter

hole punch

computer text

stickers

ribbon

brads

scoring tool

ruler

two-sided tape

embellishments (optional)

travel brochure photo

two-sided tape

- Begin the journal card with a ready-made cardstock. With deckle scissors, cut the decorative paper slightly smaller than the card face.

- Find one or more photos from your travel brochure. Cut them out with deckle scissors. (How many photos you need depends on how many card booklets you want to make.) Adhere the photo to the card face with two-sided tape.

- Borrow text from the travel brochure, create text on your computer, or write it with a calligraphy pen. Secure the text, cut to size, and adhere it to the card with two-sided tape.

- To make pages for the card journal, measure the total inside dimensions of the card. If your card measures 8½ X 5½ inches (21.5 X 14 cm), for instance, cut papers slightly shorter by about ½ inch (1.25 cm) on both sides. So paper for inside pages would measure 8 X 5 inches (20 X 12.5 cm). When folded, each page will be 5 X 4 inches (12.5 X 10 cm).

- Four paper sheets will give you eight pages to write on after they're folded. Five folded sheets will give you ten pages. For a one-week vacation, four sheets (eight booklet pages) is just right.

- Make good clean cuts with a paper cutter. Score and fold the sheets of paper pages and put them into the card fully open.

- With a hole punch, punch two holes through all layers. If this is too hard, punch holes in each layer separately, but be sure that the holes line up.

- Thread a ½-inch or thinner ribbon (allow about 2 feet or 60 cm) through the holes a few times to secure the pages to the card cover and tie a bow outside the card at the fold.

BRADS OR FASTENERS

Instead of ribbon and punched holes, you can secure pages to the card with brads or fasteners.

After inserting folded pages inside the card, close the card booklet "cover." With a hole punch or small nail, bore a hole through all layers of cardstock and paper near the fold and about 1 inch (2.5 cm) from the top. Be careful to keep your fingers out of the way.

After making your first hole, insert the brad and open its prongs on the back of the card. Still holding the layers firmly, make a second hole near the fold and about 1 inch (2.5 cm) from the card bottom. Insert the second brad and secure it.

To make the booklet easier to open when writing, score the card cover. Position a metal ruler near the fold, just beyond the brad, and use your scoring tool to score only the card cover.

HINT: You can also use lightweight card-stock sheets for the inside pages and cut them at the same size as the card cover. You can feature photos, messages, or other things inside the multipage card. Secure the pages with colorful raffia, ribbon, cord, or yarn.

Bookmark Cards

quick and easy • gift

What could be more delightful than receiving two gifts in one card? On the outside of the card is a bookmark and inside the card is a gift card to a bookstore or a new library card. Most large chain bookstores sell gift cards in different denominations. The recipient will both enjoy the book and use the bookmark you made.

Of course, if you wish, you can insert a magnetic gift card from another kind of shop, but books works well with the theme.

MATERIALS

cardstock base	hole punch
cardstock for bookmark	gift card
decorative paper	two-sided tape
ribbon	stickers

- Make a long card out of cardstock.

- Using decorative cardstock, recycled cards, or recycled gift tags, make a bookmark slightly smaller than the card cover.

- Center the bookmark over the cover of the card, and using a hole punch, punch a hole through both items.

- Thread a ribbon through the holes and tie one knot. Allow the ribbon to dangle a little.

- Inside the card, adhere the gift card to the card with stickers on all four corners of the card. They will keep the card in place. You won't want to glue or tape the back of the store gift card to the paper card if the store gift card has a magnetic strip.

Borders

BORDER LAYERS

quick and easy • fun

Borders can be created very easily by just layering decorative papers. Use contrasting colors and patterns, monochromes, or combine both techniques to make a visually appealing design.

Laugh 'til it hurts!

MATERIALS

patterned cardstock base

two-sided tape or glue stick

text

deckle scissors

decorative papers

ruler

pencil

- Use a patterned cardstock base.

- Going through scrapbook paper leftovers, you may find pretty patterns and colors. I picked out a ready-made greeting.

- Use two or more decorative papers in different sizes and layer them one on top of the other. (The card in the photo uses two.)

- To create borders, measure and mark rectangles of the desired size (each can be about 1/2 inch or 1.25 cm smaller than the other) on the back side of the decorative papers; cut out the rectangles with deckle scissors. Remove the rectangles. What remains will be framelike borders.

- With two-sided tape or a glue stick, adhere the largest border to the card face first, and then each smaller one on top. All layers create borders.

- Finally, with two-sided tape, attach a greeting.

ERASER-STAMP BORDERS
quick and easy • hand-printed

Follow directions for making an eraser-stamp from an oridinary pencil eraser on p. 46. I've shaped a square design from my eraser. By changing ink-pad colors you can make the design more interesting and colorful.

MATERIALS

cardstock base

preprinted text greeting

eraser-stamp

ink pad (several colors)

two-sided tape

- Begin with a cardstock base.
- Create a text greeting or recycle one from an old greeting card. Fasten the greeting to the center of the card with two-sided tape.
- Use an eraser-stamp loaded with ink from an ink pad to randomly print your design all around the outside edge to create your first border.
- Change ink-pad colors and create a second border around the text area by randomly stamping the design about 1/4 inch (0.63 cm) from the text box.

PAPER-BAND BORDERS

Borders just dress up a card cover like few things can. I like them because they can be simple or complex, dazzling or plain. It's up to you.

MATERIALS

cardstock base

decorative or colored paper

computer text or other text

glue stick or two-sided tape

deckle scissors

ruler

eraser-stamp print
(optional)

● Begin with cardstock base.

● Measure bands of paper about ¹/₂ inch (1.25 cm) wide, and on the underside of the decorative or colored paper, draw a light pencil line so that you'll know where to cut. With deckle scissors, cut out the four bands of paper.

● With a glue stick or two-sided tape, adhere the paper bands to the card face about ¹/₄ inch (0.63 cm) in from the edge.

● Create text on your computer or write it by hand. If you're feeling creative, snip and fray the edges of the paper with scissors. Scissors fringe cuts can be about ¹/₄ to ¹/₂ inch (0.63 to 1.25 cm) deep. Attach the text to the card with a glue stick or two-sided tape; be careful not to tape or glue the fringed parts.

Broccoli Prints
multiple cards

Broccoli may have always been an ordinary vegetable to you, but it is very pretty when used as a stamp.

Stamp ink or paint can be used to make the prints. The best bonus about broccoli stamps is that you can make multiple cards from a single slice of broccoli. Make as many as you want. If you vary the colors and embellishments, you won't tire of the design.

MATERIALS

base cardstock

fresh broccoli

kitchen paring knife

kitchen cutting board

ink pad, watercolor, or acrylic paints

artist's paintbrush

embellishments

- Using a sharp kitchen knife, carefully cut a section of broccoli lengthwise.

- Dip the broccoli in an ink pad or, using an artist's paintbrush, cover the cut flat side of the broccoli with watercolor or acrylic paint.

- Firmly press the length of broccoli to the cardstock. Carefully remove the broccoli from the cardstock.

- You may repeat this process as many times as you like.

- Embellish as desired. I've used a hole punch and inserted raffia that's tied into a bow in the front of the card.

- Discard the broccoli when you're finished. And naturally, wash your hands well before sitting down to a meal…of something else.

Bubble-Wrap Prints

BUBBLE-WRAP CARDS
handmade

Dress up the bubble-wrap prints by using deckle scissors, text appliqué, and contrasting cardstock or papers.

MATERIALS

cardstock

bubble-wrap printed paper (see p. 25)

deckle scissors

glue stick or two-sided tape

text appliqué or decal (optional)

- Choose a cardstock base.
- Cut a piece of bubble-wrap printed paper with deckle scissors, slightly smaller than the face of the card.
- With deckle scissors, cut out a smaller piece of contrasting colored paper. Make it about $1/2$ inch (1.25 cm) shorter than the bubble wrap on both sides. It could be about $1 1/4$ inches (3.25 cm) high.
- With a glue stick or two-sided tape, adhere the bubble-wrap printed paper to the front of the card (the cardstock base).
- Adhere the smaller contrasting paper to the bubble-wrap printed paper with a glue stick or two-sided tape.
- If desired, affix a greeting appliqué or decal to the paper. If you do not have a decal or appliqué, you can also use a greeting printed out from your computer in a pleasing font or one that you write by hand.

BUBBLE-WRAP PRINTED PAPER
easy • allow time

Everyone buys products cushioned in packages with bubble wrap. I like to use the smaller bubbles for hand-printed paper. If you play with colors, you can get wonderful results. This texture is easy to create, but allow time for the paint to dry. I bet your recipient will be trying to guess exactly how you created such an interesting design.

MATERIALS

cardstock base or heavy drawing paper

watercolor paint

artist's flat paintbrush (1 to 2 inches or 2.5 to 5 cm wide)

water

bubble wrap

- Be sure to use heavy drawing paper or cardstock.

- When using watercolor paint mixed with water, you must work quickly to achieve a successful result. Randomly brush paint onto the paper.

- Quickly cover the wet painted paper with the bubble wrap, bumpy bubbles down. Press firmly. Take a heavy book and put it on top of the dry side of the bubble wrap. The weight will put pressure on the bubbles, aiding the creation of the print.

- After a few hours or the next day, remove the book and bubble wrap.

HINT: If you're afraid that you'll get paint on the book or other heavy object, slip it inside a large freezer-type zipped plastic bag.

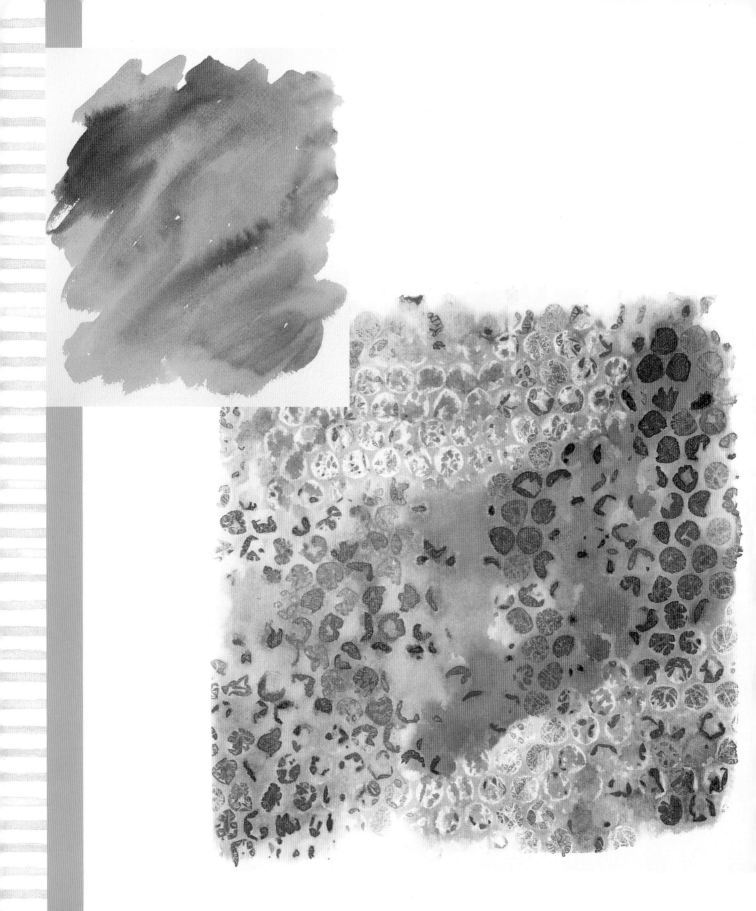

Buttons

off-the-wall • recycled

Sometimes it's fun to be a little silly. If you're like me, you have an assortment of buttons that go only with clothing you've discarded long ago. I like to collect them and recycle them into my card-making projects.

MATERIALS

colored cardstock base

decorative paper

deckle scissors

two-sided tape

assorted buttons

hard-bonding glue

hole punch

ribbon

- Use a cardstock base.
- Cut decorative paper with deckle scissors into a rectangle slightly smaller than the face of the card. Adhere it to the cardstock with two-sided tape.
- Arrange buttons in various colors and sizes on the decorative paper. When you achieve the desired design, put a little spot of glue on the decorative paper and press down on the button. Attach the remaining buttons the same way.
- Allow the glue to dry thoroughly.
- With a hole punch, make two small holes close together near the fold of the card.
- String ribbon through the holes and tie the ribbon in a bow on the front of the card.
- Mail the finished card in a padded envelope.

Clip Art

quick and easy • computer-aided • multiple cards

Clip art can be found nearly everywhere. Many computer software programs have it, and bookstores sell clip-art books (Sterling has many) that are public domain, which means that they're not copyrighted. Many pieces of clip art found in books, such as Dover's, date from the 19th century and so lend that flavor. Some books include more contemporary images. Computer clip art has a wide variety of themes. Be sure that what you're using doesn't have any copyright or trademark issues.

MATERIALS

clip art

glue stick or two-sided tape

colored or textured card-stock base

decorative paper (optional)

deckle scissors

photocopier

rhinestones, sequins, or other embellishments (optional)

hard-bonding glue (optional)

- Select clip-art designs that appeal to you.

- Cut out the designs and adhere them to cardstock or decorative paper with a glue stick or two-sided tape.

- Make a photocopy of the card on a colored or textured cardstock.

- If you wish, embellish with rhinestones or sequins, using hard-bonding glue to adhere the stones to the card.

- If you use embellishments, mail the finished card in a padded envelope.

Computer-Aided Photo Cards

computer-aided design • multiple cards

You don't have to be an artist to be able to create appealing cards. Inexpensive computer programs can achieve spectacular results. You don't even have to be especially computer savvy to fashion unique cards.

These instructions are for a PC; those for a Mac will be similar.

Adobe Photoshop is the most sophisticated and popular image and photo-manipulation software, used by professionals and amateurs alike. Adobe Photoshop Elements is a less expensive, simpler version. Other software programs can do many of the same things, and many new computers, whether Macs or PCs, come bundled with photo software.

Layout software, like Quark XPress and Adobe InDesign, also allow you to manipulate images in simple ways with color boxes, silhouettes, contorted dimensions, wrapped text, and more.

MATERIALS

cardstock base

digital or print photo and photo scanner

computer

photo manipulation software

computer color printer

laser paper

- On your computer, double-click the Adobe Photoshop or other photo icon.

- On your File menu, click Open and go to the desired folder and photo file. Or if you have a photo on a CD, go to the disk drive on your computer to open the CD where you've stored a photo or other picture that you want to work with. (On a Mac, the CD icon will appear on the desktop.) Double-click the file to open it or simply click "open" after you've selected the appropriate file from your photo file list.

- Before you do anything to the photo or other image, save it under a new name. You do that by clicking on the File menu, and selecting "Save as." You can even save it in a new folder. That way you'll keep the original photo clean in case you don't like your results and want to start fresh.

- Go to Filter on the menu bar. When the Filter menu bar drops down, you'll have lots of options. You can blur, stylize, sharpen, and do lots of things. Play around and see what effects you like.

- See examples of how you can alter a photo that shows a row of deck chairs on p. 31. Our photo software computer options created colored pencil, cutout, stained glass, ocean, pallette knife, and poster edges.

- After you find what you like, click on OK. Save the image.

- Click on the File menu and then click the Printer Setup option. Choose the paper size and orientation you want to print. For orientation, the portrait option gives you more height than width, and the landscape option allows more width than height.

- Choose the size and number of altered photos you want to print.

- Click on Print (or OK).

Original

(Filter, Artistic) Colored Pencil

(Filter, Artistic) Cutout

(Filter, Texture) Stained Glass

(Filter, Distort) Ocean Ripple

(Filter, Artistic) Poster Edges

Cutouts
fun • challenging

If flowers will make you smile...

...then here's a bunch so smile a lot

Cutouts in the cover or face of the card partially reveal what's inside the card. These cutouts can be in many small shapes or be themselves large windows to reveal an image or message inside. (Also see Windows on p. 151.)

MATERIALS

cardstock base

craft knife

cutting mat

flowers photo

computer or handwritten text

green marking pen

two-sided tape or glue stick

- Begin with cardstock base.

- On the inside of the card, adhere a photo of flowers using two-sided tape or a glue stick.

- On the card cover, with the card open, cut the shape of a flower in the middle of the card. When the card is closed, part of the floral photo should show through the cover's cutout or window. If you wish, cut a hole or window where the flowers on the photo will show. With a green marking pen, draw a stem and leaf on the cover coming out of the cutout flower.

- Write one to three cheerful lines with computer or handwritten text. Have one part of the text on the cover of the card and use the rest inside the card. For a little more interest, instead of cutting the text paper, tear it by hand, and adhere it to the card with a glue stick.

Decals
quick and easy

In most craft, art, and stationery stores you'll find a wealth of decals and decorative papers to use for card-making.

If your recipient has a hobby or occupation, decals are most likely available with the appropriate images or themes. Most decals are self-sticking, which makes your job easier. The fun is selecting decals and decorative papers to mix and match.

MATERIALS

cardstock base

decals

decorative paper(s)

glue stick or two-sided tape

deckle scissors

embellishments (optional)

- Use a contrasting or coordinating card base, or cover the cardstock base completely with decorative paper.

- Cut a piece of decorative paper with a paper cutter or craft knife if you want a straight edge, or use deckle scissors if you'd prefer a decorative edge.

- Adhere the decorative paper to the cardstock with two-sided tape or a glue stick.

- Adhere decals to the decorative paper using a glue stick or two-sided tape if the decals are not preglued.

- Embellish as desired.

- Mail delicate finished cards in a padded envelope.

Deckle Edges
quick and easy

Depending on what you do with your scissor cuts, deckle edges could work for a jagged Halloween message, rounded scallops for a fancy and lacy valentine, watery waves for a bon voyage, egg-and-darts for an Art Nouveau appearance, kid cuts for a child's birthday, or an odd assortment of cuts for humorous cards.

A simple vertical or horizontal cut along one edge of your paper may be all you need. Deckle edges, depending on the kind and the materials you use, can make any card go from plain to fancy, simple to formal, or just-OK to something on the wild side.

Here are a few hints.

- Most deckle scissors have a "repeat" pattern. When making a long continuous cut, it is best to match up the repeat. If the pattern is random, there won't be a problem.

- Cut the front right edge of the card with deckle, revealing the usual straight card edge below.

- It's OK to use any paper, foil, or cardstock as long as the deckle scissors can make a clean cut. Very thin foil or rice paper will not cut well. Corrugated stock would not be suitable. Drawing a light pencil line would help guide your cutting.

- Cut your paper or cardstock in a position in which you are comfortable. I usually hold my paper off my work table. You may be more comfortable cutting on the table. Aside from straight cuts, you can be creative and cut at angles, curves, random shapes, circles, measured, or freestyle. The creation can be as simple as cutting one edge, or you can get carried away and make lots of cuts with different deckle edges all on one card.

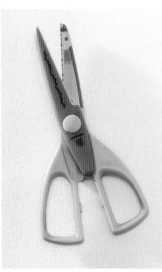

Decorative Papers
quick and easy

You can quickly and easily create a card using simply a cardstock base and decorative paper or even leftover wrapping paper. A quick cut with deckle scissors and you'll have the card face ready for your message.

MATERIALS

cardstock base

decorative paper or wrapping paper

deckle scissors

two-sided tape

embellishment (optional)

message (ink on paper or computer-generated)

- Begin with cardstock base.

- Using deckle scissors, cut a square or rectangle of decorative paper or wrapping paper a little smaller than the card face.

- With two-sided tape, adhere the decorative paper to the front of the card.

- Carefully position and adhere your message to the decorative paper with two-sided tape.

- Add any embellishments desired.

Die-Cuts
quick and easy • elegant simplicity

Combine the use of die-cuts with fabulous colored cardstock and decorative papers, and you have a winning card design. Or you can use dramatic black-and-white cardstock. Your friends and family will be impressed. This is one card that a home computer and printer cannot make!

Die-cuts are inexpensive and can be found in arts and crafts stores. They punch small decorative holes in paper and cardstock. You'll find many designs to choose from, such as music notes, flowers, butterflies, snowflakes, hearts, and more. Corner die-cut devices usually have built-in guides to help you correctly position the paper or cardstock.

MATERIALS
cardstock base

decorative or colored paper

die-cut

deckle scissors

two-sided tape or glue stick

embellishment (optional)

- Use a ready-made cardstock or cut your own.

- Cut decorative or colored papers with a deckle edge into rectangular or square shapes.

- Use a die-cut to make the desired design in the paper rectangles or squares. Adhere the decorative paper to the cardstock with a glue stick or two-sided tape. Layer one or more papers on the cardstock. You'll want to use contrasting colors so that the die-cut or cutout appears clean and clear against the second color background.

- Embellish as desired.

Embossed Cards

EMBOSSING PROCESS
moderately challenging

Embossed cardstock is readily available; you can make attractive cards very quickly with it. Although making your own embossed cards is a little more challenging, the results are well worth it. You'll need to buy a stencil, cardstock, and stylus. When using a stencil, a light box is usually necessary to work on your design.

Or simply find an embossing kit with all the tools you'll need contained neatly in one box. A kit eliminates the need for a light box. An embossing kit also makes it easier to line up desired motifs. For this card, I've used a kit.

MATERIALS

cardstock base

paper

embossing kit or tools (stencils, stylus, working surface, pegs to hold stencils)

letter and other embossing stencils

light box (optional)

two-sided tape

glue stick

- Begin with letter stencils.

- Using the guidelines that are on the embossing stencil, place the cardstock upside down over the reversed stencil. A reversed stencil will have the letters upside down also. The reason for this is that when you rub the stylus in the motif, the embossing will come out correctly when finished. The embossing is pushing the cardstock or paper forward and away from you. When turned around, the embossed surface will be raised.

- Position the cardstock or paper over the first letter you want to work with. Once in place, use your stylus to firmly press down on the image in the stencil. Work around the edges and then move to the middle of the letter.

- When finished, move the cardstock to another letter and repeat the first process. Use the guidelines to keep the letters in line. Or you can put the letters at an angle for a different look.

- After you complete the letters, add a border.

- Change the stencil and use one with lines, designs, and borders. A wavy line was used in this design. When I finished the bottom line, below my letters, I moved the cardstock to position the wavy line above the letters.

- After doing all this, I wanted to add a little more pizzazz. So I used a stencil with dots. I kept moving my cardstock to position the dots along the wavy lines.

LAYERING WITH EMBOSSED CARDSTOCK

- Use a colorful cardstock base.

- With regular or deckle scissors, cut colorful embossed cardstock slightly smaller than the cardstock base. Adhere the embossed cardstock to the cardstock base with two-sided tape or a glue stick.

- Arrange appliqués on top of the embossed cardstock if desired.

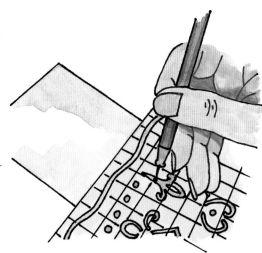

Using a stylus to emboss a shape onto cardstock.

HINT: You can create an elegant card made with ivory-colored cardstock and just embossing.

MONOGRAM WITH COLOR EMBOSSING
moderately challenging

This isn't your grandmother's monogram. Take a classic monogram and turn it modern with the "in" colors of the year. This design uses hot pink, orange, and lime. Add a little die-cut and deckle edge for a little more zip to the design.

MATERIALS

cardstock base

colored paper

embossing kit

die-cut motif

two-sided tape

glue stick

deckle scissors

hole punch

paper cutter

- Using colored paper, emboss the word LOVE into one colored paper. Follow the embossing directions on p. 38.

- Cut out the word with deckle scissors. This piece measures 1$\frac{1}{2}$ x 3$\frac{1}{2}$ inches (about 4 x 9 cm).

- Using a second colored paper, emboss a decorative line. A wavy line was used here. The parallel lines are spaced about 2 inches (5 cm) apart. Cut out this paper on a paper cutter to measure 2$\frac{1}{2}$ x 4 inches (6 x 10 cm).

- With two-sided tape, adhere the LOVE paper to the wavy-line paper.

- Adhere the assembled papers askew to a base cardstock that's about 5 x 4$\frac{1}{4}$ inches (12.5 x 11 cm). Use two-sided tape.

- Using a flower die-cut, cut out two flowers in paper.

- With a hole punch, cut a center hole in the flowers. Adhere the flowers to the cardstock with a glue stick.

READY-MADE EMBOSSED FRAME CARD
quick and easy

Embossed cardstocks are sensual to the touch. The raised design is usually the same color as the cardstock, while the embossed surface reflects light and shadows. Your cards can be elegant or fun, depending on what you do with your creativity.

Embossed designs go nicely with other card-making techniques, too. Embossed cardstock makes an attractive frame for art or a photo.

MATERIALS

embossed cardstock base

art or photo

scissors or deckle scissors

two-sided tape or glue stick

one-sided tape (optional)

● Choose a cardstock with a subtle embossed design.

● Cut out a piece of art or use a photograph for the center of the card. If you wish, cut a deckle edge on the art or photo.

● With a glue stick or two-sided tape, adhere the art or photo to the embossed cardstock.

HINT: You can also use an embossed mat or frame and adhere it to the cardstock with two-sided tape or a glue stick. First tape the photo or artwork facedown to the back of the mat or frame. Then mount the photo and frame on the cardstock with two-sided tape.

Envelopes

DIE-CUT ENVELOPE FLAPS
quick and easy

Die-cuts come in a variety of shapes. You'll find stars, flowers, leaves, geometric shapes, hearts, snowflakes, shamrocks, and much more. The smaller die-cuts will allow you to suggest constellations of stars or a mini-snowstorm. Larger ones may be easier to manage and suit kids' projects. You could choose the child's initial(s) or a simple boat, plane, car, cat, or dog.

MATERIALS

envelope

die-cut(s)

colored paper

one-sided tape

- Holding the envelope steady, punch your die-cut design into the envelope's flap.

- On the inside of the flap, cover the newly punched hole(s) with contrasting colored paper cut to size. Using one-sided tape, adhere the paper to the envelope's flap.

- When you close the flap you'll see a cutout with colored paper showing through.

HINT: Experiment with the effects of individual die-cuts on inexpensive test paper (we use photocopier paper or even newsprint) before committing your design to an envelope. Of course, a single die-cut window added to an envelope (or indeed a card) may be all you need.

HANDMADE ENVELOPES

challenging • fits any card size

Since you're fashioning your own card, you may have odd sizes that don't quite fit existing envelopes. Here's how you can create your own envelope to fit any card size.

MATERIALS

paper for envelope

ruler

pencil

craft knife

cutting mat or cardboard

two-sided tape or glue stick

decal, sticker, or melted-wax sealing tools (optional)

- For an average-size card, you'll need at least a 12 x 12-inch (30 x 30-cm) sheet of paper. To make an envelope for a really large card, you may need to use paper that comes on a roll or find another thin (not as heavy as cardstock) oversized paper. Directions here will suit an envelope that fits on large scrapbook paper.

- Measure with a ruler and mark the areas for the card, top, bottom, and side flaps with your pencil. See the diagram and note particulars below. You'll be drawing light pencil lines that you'll then cut out.

- Keep in mind that the area reserved for the card needs to be a little larger than the card itself. Allow extra space at the top and on one side: 3/8 inch (1 cm), or about the thickness of a pencil.

- Make the bottom flap shorter than the card by about 3/4 inch (2 cm), or the width of your thumb.

- Make the pointy V-shaped top flap half the height of the card area.

- For the smaller side flaps, measure parallel to the envelope sides about 3/4 inch (2 cm) or the width of your thumb. Draw a light pencil line from top to bottom.

- With your craft knife, cut along your drawn outline of the envelope. (See the solid line in the diagram.)

- Score the rectangle or square area reserved for your card on the marked and printed side. (See the dotted line in the diagram.)

- To make folding and gluing easier, clip a little angle off the **side flaps'** four corners. Fold in the sides and apply glue or two-sided tape. Then fold the **bottom flap** up and secure it with two-sided tape or glue.

- We want a **pointed top flap**. Find the center of the top flap (top, outer edge) and mark it lightly with your pencil. Measure up from the card area (see dotted line in diagram) on each side of the top flap 1¼ inches (3 cm), or about the width of two fingers, and mark these spots. To create the pointed flap, using a craft knife and ruler, cut away from the left side to the center point and from the right side to the center point. And you're done.

- If you'd prefer a more decorative top flap, cut the edges forming the point with deckle scissors.

- Insert the card into the finished envelope. Fold the top flap down. Secure the top flap with a decal, sticker, glue, or two-sided tape. If you want it to be fancy, use melted-wax seal with the desired impression.

HINTS: Remember that less weighty envelopes and cards are less expensive to send abroad. If you don't want to make a V-shaped flap, you could use 8½ X 11-inch (21.5 X 28 cm or A4) paper to create an envelope with a square or rounded flap.

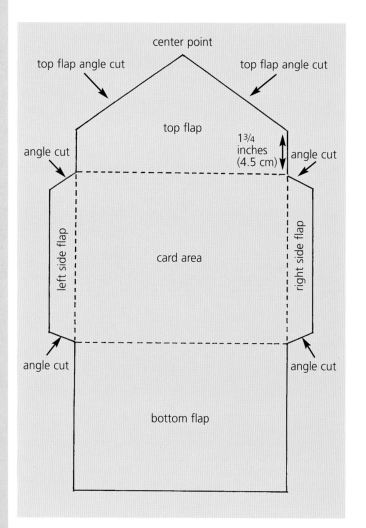

LININGS FOR ENVELOPES AND FLAPS
recycled paper

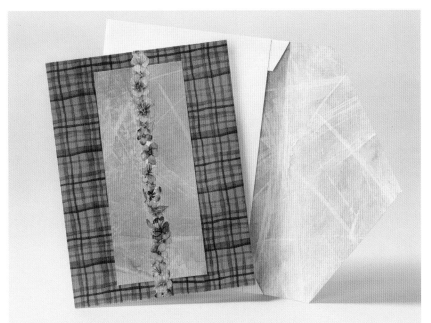

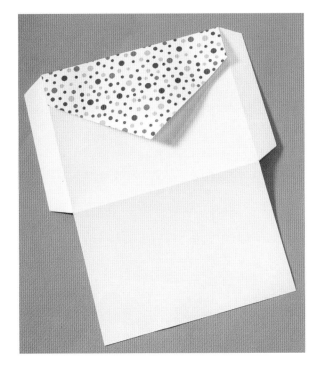

- Select a V-shaped flap envelope that will fit your finished card.
- With deckle scissors, cut V-shaped decorative papers to fit the flap.
- With a glue stick, completely cover the underside of the decorative papers.
- Place decorative paper on the inside of the envelope flap, making sure that it's smooth. Make sure that the flap is dry and that no excess glue oozes out. Cut the edge of the decorative-paper flap with deckle scissors.

LININGS FOR ENVELOPES

The procedure for lining envelopes begins with a flat, not-yet-folded envelope. Simply use a glue stick to adhere the decorative paper to the flat, unfolded envelope paper, then fold, shape, and create the envelope as you normally would. Another option would be to use decorative paper that's printed on one side and plain on the outside. (See Handmade Envelopes on pp. 43–44.)

Eraser-Stamps

quick and easy

MAKING THE ERASER-STAMP

From an ordinary pencil eraser, we can create our own inky "stamps." Try using your eraser-stamp with one or more ink stamp pads (having different colors is nice); you'll be all set to have fun.

MATERIALS

pencil with clean "new" eraser tip
craft or X-acto knife

- Cut a triangle, square, hexagon, circle, or other shape into an unused pencil eraser. Or use the eraser as-is for a dot motif.

- With a sharp craft knife, carefully cut away from the eraser tip what you do not want printed. For the triangle, make one clean cut down from the top of the eraser on each of the three sides, turning the eraser for each cut. Slice down to the metal band. Remove excess eraser parts.

  - One way is to cut vertically down the eraser from the top and then remove the excess by cutting in, horizontally, near the metal band from the side.

- Another way is to insert the knife back into the three cuts and twist the knife blade away from the center and toward the eraser's outside edge.

- As you become more practiced, you'll be able to make more shallow cuts in the eraser (see drawing), which will give your eraser stamp more stability.

HINT: Avoid using old, hard, and brittle erasers. They do not easily absorb or transfer ink.

CAUTION: Craft or X-acto knives are very sharp. To protect your hand from cuts, make a cardboard shield about 4 inches (10 cm) square. Cut a small hole in the center and slide the pencil through it. Hold the pencil underneath the shield while you use the other hand to cut and shape the eraser.

USING THE ERASER-STAMP

You'll figure out lots of ways to dress up cards with eraser-stamp borders and other geometric images.

White envelopes are fine, but even a little bit of color can be fabulous. Make a bold design statement by embellishing your envelopes with unique stamped designs that you've created. Dress up that padded envelope, too.

MATERIALS

eraser-stamp

ink stamp pad(s)

cardstock base or plain paper

plain or padded envelope

● After you've made your pencil eraser-stamp, you can begin printing. You may want to practice a little on scrap paper or newspaper.

● Dip the eraser in an ink pad and then press it firmly onto the card or envelope. Use multiple colors or metallic ink for variety.

● What's great is that the eraser-stamp will last a long time.

HINTS: Play with random printing. You can also make stripes, plaids, waves, lines, and other patterns with eraser prints. Let your children have a go at it, too. Use other shapes on another card or envelope. The more the merrier. You may want to avoid stamping in the area on the envelope where you'll put the postage stamp; some inks may prevent the stamp glue from sticking completely.

Flowers

feminine

Combine silk flowers with decorative paper to create a lovely feminine card for a female friend, cousin, sister, mom, aunt, or grandmother.

MATERIALS

silk flower

raffia or ribbon

cardstock

decorative papers

two-sided tape or glue stick

hole punch

deckle scissors (optional)

- Select a pretty colored cardstock.

- With deckle or other scissors, cut a contrasting piece of decorative paper slightly smaller than the front of the card.

- With a glue stick or two-sided tape, adhere the paper to the front of the cardstock.

- Cut a second decorative paper slightly smaller than the first paper, and adhere it with a glue stick or two-sided tape to the first decorative paper. If you wish, you can use deckle scissors on decorative paper.

- Use a hole punch to make two small holes near each other on the front of the card where you want to secure the small silk flower or silk flowers bouquet.

- Thread raffia or ribbon through the holes and tie small silk flower(s) to the card.

- Finish with a bow.

- Mail the card in a padded envelope.

Foam Appliqués
quick and easy

Foam appliqués can be found at most craft shops. They're usually self-sticking. Match the appliqués with appropriate decorative paper, and you'll have a winner. I've used a beach towel and flip-flops to suggest a lazy summer theme. For another I chose a cat and dog with suggestive paw prints. The third card shows embossed cardstock with subtle swirls echoed in the foam-appliqué swirls and the dragonfly appliqué.

MATERIALS

cardstock base

decorative paper

foam appliqués

glue stick

deckle scissors

tag (optional)

brads (optional)

- Use a firm cardstock (embossed, if you wish) when working with foam appliqués because they're thick and a little heavier than most paper and other objects you'd want to glue to the cardstock.

- Find decorative paper with a theme that complements the appliqué. (You could try handmade salt paper.) Using deckle scissors, cut the decorative paper slightly smaller than the cover of the card.

- Adhere the decorative paper to the front of the cardstock with a glue stick or two-sided tape.

- Position the foam appliqués on the decorative paper, remove the paper backing, reposition them, and press down, making sure that they stick securely. If you wish, add a tag, securing it with brads.

- Mail the finished card in a padded envelope.

Formal-Dress Cards

sophisticated • black and gold

Just as a little black dress or indeed a tuxedo with tails appears elegant and sophisticated, black greeting cards can, too. Ordinary paper will not do here; we'll need something unique. A little bit of gold paper or gold foil will enhance the look. We've also added a little rice paper. This will surely bring appreciative sighs. Send this card for that formal or fancy-dress occasion.

Rice paper, often handmade in a variety of designs, can be found at most arts and crafts stores.

MATERIALS

black cardstock base

deckle scissors

two-sided tape

gold paper

handmade rice paper

gold ink pen (optional)

- Begin with a black cardstock base.

- With deckle scissors, cut the cover of the card slightly shorter than the back of the card.

- Keep your deckle scissors handy by cutting gold paper slightly larger than the piece you've removed from the front of the card.

- Adhere the gold paper to the inside bottom edge of the card using two-sided tape.

- Cut another piece of gold paper for the front of the card and put it aside.

- Cut or tear off a piece of rice paper.

- Adhere the rice paper to the cover of the card with two-sided tape.

- Using two-sided tape, place the reserved gold paper on top of the rice paper.

- Write your greeting on the inside of the card with a gold ink pen. If you choose not to use the gold ink pen, you could instead paste white paper on the inside of the card so that you'll have a place to write your message in ordinary ink. You can give that white paper a deckle edge as well to create a more elegant look.

- Top this off with an envelope with a gold-foil interior; you'll find one in a stationery store. If not, make your own (see Envelopes).

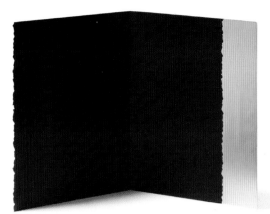

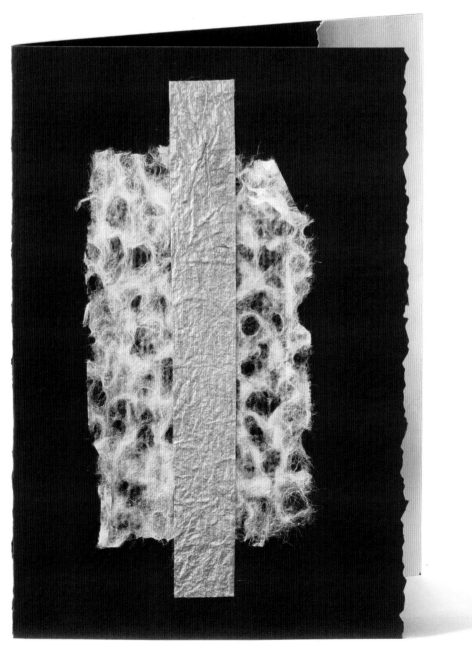

Frames

MAKING YOUR OWN FRAME
challenging

If you want to start from scratch, you can make your own frame in desired proportions or sizes. For sharp, clean cuts, we advise using a metal ruler, X-acto blade, and a cutting mat.

MATERIALS

metal ruler

pencil

triangle tool or
T square

colored cardboard or
stiff paper for frame

cutting mat or card-
board (to protect
work surface)

craft knife (or X-acto
knife)

- Decide what size you want the frame to be on the outside.

- Using your triangle or T square and a pencil, draw a right angle on the colored cardboard.

- You now have two straight sides.

- Measure one side to be the long side of the frame and put a pencil mark along the line.

- Measure the other side and put a pencil mark at the end of the dimension you want.

- Using one side of the triangle, align the edge closely along one of the lines and at the pencil mark you drew.

- Draw a line for the third side of the frame.

- Line up the triangle to the other line at the pencil mark and draw the fourth side of the frame.

- When you've determined the outside dimension, you can cut it out with your craft knife.

- With your ruler, measure 1 inch (2.54 cm) in from each side and draw a pencil line.

- Using your craft knife and ruler, cut out the hole of the frame.

- Do all your cutting on thick cardboard or a craft cutting mat to protect your work table.

FRAME TEMPLATE

Although you can use ready-made frames and photo borders to create cards, it's nice to make your own frames from scratch. Give that special photo a good turn by fashioning your own individual frame. Draw on a theme that coordinates with the photo.

If the photo tells a big fish story, for instance, your frame could be embossed or otherwise decorated with imaginary lures, fishes, boats, or fishing lines.

● The template measures 5 x 7 inches (about 12.5 x 17.8 cm). Photocopy the template to adjust it to the desired size. After you've figured out what size you want, make a template out of thin cardboard. Use this cardboard template as a pattern for future projects. With a pencil, trace the pattern onto the cardstock, and with a craft knife, cut out the frame and hole. Be sure to cover your work table with heavy cardboard, a cutting board, or a craft mat to protect it from damage.

PHOTO-FRAME CARDS
quick and easy

Photo Greeting Card
Suitable for
3 1/2" x 5" or 4" x 6" photo

You want to send a photo to a friend or family member, but you'd like to dress it up. Many card and photo supply shops sell ready-made photo frame cards. You'll find them in standard sizes to fit 3 × 5-inch or 4 × 6-inch photos or the appropriate centimeter equivalents (roughly 7.5 × 12.5 cm or 10 × 15 cm). Many are designed for holidays or special occasions.

MATERIALS

photo-frame cards

photo

- Slide your photo into the slot provided to accommodate a photo. The photo should fit snugly in place. Glue or tape should not be necessary.

- Write your own personal greeting inside the card. Many holiday cards come with printed greetings.

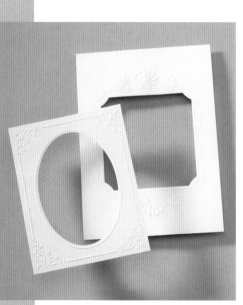

DOILY FRAME

MATERIALS

frame-card base

frame template

square or rectangular doily

photo or print

two-sided tape

one-sided tape

scissors

craft knife

metal ruler or triangle tool

stickers (optional)

- Use your own template to make the frame-card base or use a ready-made frame-card base.

- With a square or rectangular doily, cut out the decorative lacy edge with a craft knife and ruler.

The doily will need to be larger than the hole of your frame to allow for trimming. Work with a metal ruler and a sharp craft knife on heavy cardboard or a cutting mat to protect your work table. Cut along the decorative edge of lace all around the rectangle or square. Cut two opposite diagonal corners and separate. Position over the frame and trim excess length.

Use two-sided tape to adhere the lacy doily to the frame card.

Turn the frame over and adhere a photo or print to the back of the frame using one-sided tape.

Apply stickers to the front of the frame if desired. You can overlap the stickers with the photo or print.

Cut doily with a craft knife and a ruler or triangle tool.

FOIL-FRAME CARDS

Ready-made blank foil cards, some with frames, can be elegant. They're found in craft or office supply stores. Share your favorite photo with friends or recycle an old greeting card inside a foil frame.

MATERIALS

foil photo-frame card or foil-edge cardstock

photo or recycled card

two-sided tape

deckle scissors (optional)

● Select a ready-made foil photo-frame card.

● Position the photo or recycled greeting card in the opening of the foil card and secure it with two-sided tape if the frame is not constructed so that it will hold it in place.

HINT: Foil can become a decorative element in card-making. Use it as a shaped snippet, layer, or frame. Depending on its weight, foil can be delicate to work with.

Gift Pack of Greeting Cards

multiple cards • feminine

I enjoy making four cards that are all the same and then packaging them as a gift. They are especially good for hostess gifts. This project is made with hydrangea paper and silk-flower embellishment. I used hydrangeas because they're the favorite flower of the recipient. You can choose a flower for this gift card that's your friend's favorite.

MATERIALS

cardstock

decorative paper

deckle scissors

two-sided tape or glue stick

raffia

silk flower

- Start with a cardstock base.
- Using deckle scissors, cut a floral decorative paper.
- Adhere the paper to the cardstock with a glue stick or two-sided tape.
- Make four cards all the same.
- Stack four envelopes and stack the four cards on top of the envelopes.
- Wrap the bundle with raffia.
- Place a silk flower in the knot of the raffia and tie a bow.
- Mail the finished card pack in a padded envelope or take them with you when you visit your friend.

Gift Tags

Gift tags are usually smaller than greeting and note cards. That's of course because they're usually attached to a gift, big or small. They can be simple or highly decorative. Here we show a variety of gift tags; some include envelopes.

Assorted gift tags

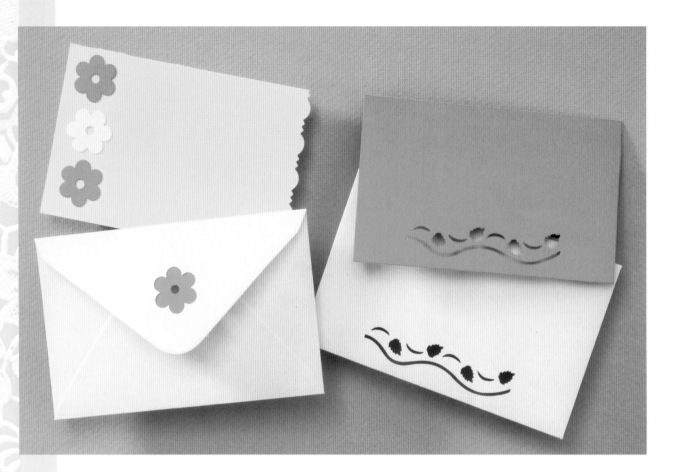

DIE-CUT GIFT TAGS AND ENVELOPES

MATERIALS

cardstock or cardstock scraps

tiny envelope(s)

die-cut

colored paper

glue stick

deckle scissors

hole punch

one-sided tape

- Use a colorful cardstock cut to the desired size. To make the simple gift cards or gift tags a little more dressy, cut one of the edges with deckle scissors.

- Using a flower design die-cut, cut out a flower in a different color paper than that of the cardstock itself. If you wish, you could make several flowers, each in a different color for a little bouquet.

- Cut a small hole in the center of each flower with the hole punch.

- Adhere the flowers to the cardstock by using a glue stick on the back of the flower(s).

- With a die-cut, cut out a flower on the flap of the envelope.

- Cut a small piece of colored paper and tape it to the inside of the envelope flap so that it shows through your cutout.

GIFT TAGS FROM SCRAPS

If you have many pieces of cardstock scraps left over from larger projects, don't let them go to waste. Recycle them. Make small gift tags. Dress them up with embellishments.

MATERIALS

cardstock scrap(s)

recycled gift tag

deckle scissors

raffia

rhinestone(s)

two-sided tape

hard-bonding glue

hole punch

- Cut a cardstock scrap to size.
- Using deckle scissors, cut an old gift tag.
- Adhere the gift tag to the cardstock with two-sided tape.
- Make sure the card is flat on your work table.
- Using hard-bonding glue, dab a very small amount of the glue onto the back of the rhinestone.
- Place the rhinestone in the corner of the gift tag. Do the same with all four corners.
- Let the glue dry according to the instructions.
- Punch a hole in the upper left corner of the folded card.
- Thread raffia through the hole and tie a knot. Leave enough raffia to tie it to a package.

GIFT TAGS WITH GLITTERY STICKERS

Use stickers to create a wonder gift tag. This project uses a glitter sticker and will dress up any gift.

MATERIALS

cardstock

glitter sticker

hole punch

ribbon

deckle scissors

● With deckle scissors, cut your cardstock to the desired size for the gift tag.

● Place the self-sticking glitter sticker on the cardstock gift tag.

● Using the hole punch, punch a hole in the upper left corner of the card. Be sure to punch all the way through the front and back covers of the card.

● Thread a ribbon through the hole and tie a bow.

● If you want to attach this card to the ribbon of a package, loop the card's ribbon through the ribbon on the package and then tie the final package-ribbon bow.

GIFT TAGS WITH STICKERS

MATERIALS

cardstock

recycled cards or stickers

yarn

two-sided tape or glue stick

deckle scissors

hole punch

● Cut a small card base from cardstock.

● Cut an old card, calendar, or other image using deckle scissors. Cut the image slightly smaller than the cover of your card.

● Adhere the old card or calendar image with two-sided tape or a glue stick.

● Using a hole punch, punch a hole in the top left corner of the folded card. Let the hole go through the cover and back of the card.

● Thread decorative yarn through the hole and tie a knot. Leave enough yarn to tie the tag to a gift.

Glitter

pizzazz

Is there anything with more pizzazz than glitter? You can add glitter to almost anything and it can look— depending on the color scheme and other elements—feminine and fancy, glitzy, or jazzy.

MATERIALS

cardstock base

die-cut

deckle scissors

decorative paper

colored paper

glitter

glue pen

two-sided tape or glue stick

- Begin with a cardstock base.

- With deckle scissors, cut out an interesting shape of colored paper.

- Adhere the colored paper shape to the cardstock base with two-sided tape or a glue stick.

- Cut out decorative paper with deckle scissors. Punch a die-cut design into the decorative paper.

- With two-sided tape or a glue stick, carefully position and adhere the die-cut decorative paper on top of the colored paper.

- Make designs on the card face with a glue pen. Quickly sprinkle glitter onto the glue and let dry a few moments.

- Shake off the extra glitter onto a paper and funnel it back into the container. There's no point in wasting glitter; you may want it for another project.

Hangings

BUTTERFLY "STAINED-GLASS" HANGING
challenging • gift

Many printed vellum designs work nicely with suncatchers and other hangings. This design is a stained-glass pattern. The design of red stained-glass butterflies contrasts with the blue parchment cardstock base. The stylized butterfly shape is easy to cut with a craft knife. Hang this in a window when it's snowing outside to remind you of the joys of summer butterflies fluttering in the breeze.

MATERIALS

long cardstock (not folded)	hole punch
parchment cardstock	ribbon
glue stick	ruler
craft knife	cutting mat
stained-glass vellum pattern	paper cutter
blue marker	pencil
black marker	tracing paper
computer or handwritten text	light box (or sunny window)

- Cut out a long piece of cardstock on your paper cutter. The finished card measures 5 × 8½ inches (12.7 × 21.5 cm); it will be flat and not folded.

- Cut the vellum slightly smaller than the cardstock.

- With a pencil, draw a butterfly on tracing paper. After you've drawn the size and shape you want, go over the lines with a black marker so you can see them when transferring the design to the cardstock.

- Use a light box or sunny window to trace the design onto the cardstock with a pencil.

- Cut the design out with a craft knife on a cutting mat (to protect your work table and to ensure clean cuts).

- After your butterfly cutouts are finished, adhere the vellum to the back side of the cardstock that has pencil markings. Use a glue stick to cover the cardstock so that it bonds with the vellum.

- By hand or on your computer, write the words butterfly in different languages. Cut the printouts into geometric shapes with a craft knife and ruler. Attach them to the card face with a glue stick.

- Draw the butterflies' antennae with a blue marking pen.

- On the top center of the card, punch a hole with your hole punch that's about ½ inch (1.25 cm) into the cardstock.

- Thread a ribbon through the hole and tie a bow. The card can now be hung in the window from the ribbon.

HINT: This flat card does not require a back unless you'd like to add one to cover your work. If you add a decorative paper back, be sure to cut out the appropriate windows for the butterflies so that the sun or light can shine through.

Treat the finished suncatcher as a postcard that's mailed in an envelope.

SUNCATCHER
challenging • gift

Your friend will be able to hang this suncatcher in a window to enjoy for a long time. The length of this suncatcher card should be double the width.

I love beads and prisms in a sunny window because I enjoy watching the dancing rainbows they cast on my walls.

MATERIALS

corrugated cardstock (not folded)

craft knife

cutting mat or heavy cardboard (to protect table)

printed vellum

one-sided tape

two-sided tape

computer or handwritten text

hole punch

solid-colored cardstock (not folded)

deckle scissors

scissors

brads

string of beads

raffia

ruler

pencil

- With a craft knife, cut out from the corrugated cardstock the desired card shape and hole. Use heavy cardboard or a cutting mat to protect your table.

- Cut the decorative vellum a little larger than the hole in the corrugated cardstock. Tape the vellum to the back of the card with one-sided tape. Do not let the tape show in the hole.

- Write text by hand (here's where calligraphy would come in handy) or on your computer in a pleasing type font. Cut out the printed message with deckle scissors.

- Using deckle scissors, cut out solid-colored cardstock a little larger than the text. Adhere the text to the cardstock with two-sided tape. Fasten the text assembly to the front of the corrugated card with brads in each corner.

- With a hole punch, make two holes on the top corners of the card. Thread raffia through the holes and tie a bow. The raffia can be hung on a hook in a window.

- On the back side of the card, run a row of two-sided tape near the bottom edge of the card.

- Hang a short string of beads across the bottom of the card. Press the band of beads onto the two-sided tape. Cover this with one-sided tape to secure the beads.

Mail the finished card in a padded envelope.

HINT: If the back of the light-catcher card will be visible as it sways in the breeze, cover the back of the card with decorative or plain paper cut to size and secured with two-sided tape. Of course, you'll need to make a cutout in the decorative paper for the light-catching window in the corrugated card. Use the template again as needed.

The flowers
Are smiling
For you
Today.

Initials
quick and easy

Here's something personal. Create an elegant card that bears your friend or family member's initial (first or last name). Of course, the surname initial creates a more formal card. The style of the initial and its placement will also make a difference as to whether it's formal or fun.

Rhinestones will be glitzy, but elegant script or calligraphy plus a more sedate background will make the cards appear more formal.

Make the initial large or small, depending on your taste and overall design.

MATERIALS

ready-made decorative cardstock

decorative or solid paper

decorative calligraphy or computer-printed initial

deckle scissors or regular scissors

two-sided tape or glue stick

rhinestone (optional)

hard-bonding glue

- Using a ready-made card will save time.
- Create fancy calligraphy with a calligraphic marker or calligraphy pen.
- Or instead, choose a fancy type font from your computer type manager. Make it really big, say from 26 to 72 points or larger. (The letter M on the card shown is 55 points, but apparent point size can vary with the type font.) Print it out. You may find that you need to enlarge it on a photocopier machine. Adjust the initial's size for the appearance and design you want for the given card.
- With deckle or other scissors, cut out the initial from the computer printout. Cut a rectangle or square around the initial. Or, if you wish, make a silhouette; cut around the outline of the initial itself. (If you're using calligraphy paper, adjust the size of the calligraphy paper by cutting away any excess.) Adhere the initial to decorative or solid paper with two-sided tape or a glue stick.
- Adhere the assembled pieces to decorative cardstock.
- Put a little dab of hard-bonding glue on the bottom of a rhinestone. Position the rhinestone on the card. Let dry.
- Mail the finished card in a padded envelope.

OPTION: You could also use two or three initials. If you use three, make the initial for the last name large and the other two, on either side of the large initial, about two-thirds or half as big.

HINT: If you enlarge calligraphy on a photocopier it will not appear as crisp. You can reduce but not enlarge calligraphy, for best results. Usually we advise that you not reduce it by more than 25 percent.

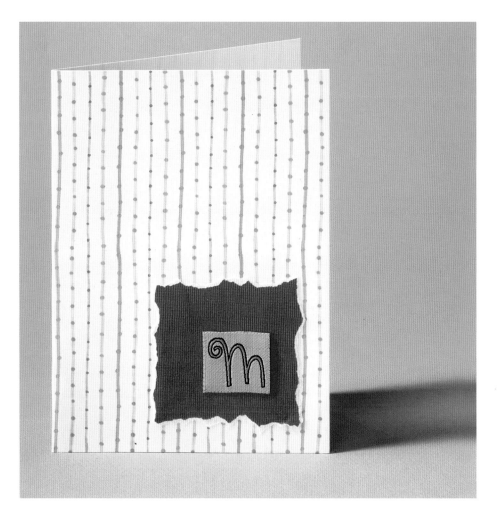

Ink Prints
fun

Bottled ink comes in vivid colors; it's easy to use. If you've been saving somewhat flat seashells, such as scallop shells, for a special project, try this.

MATERIALS

heavy cardstock or watercolor paper

artist's large paintbrush

artist's small round #4 to #6 paintbrush

2 shallow plastic or foam cups

deep blue ink

turquoise ink

hard-bonding glue

seashells

HINT: Try different colors of ink and designs. You can glue various found objects to the ink-print card.

- You can use the ink right out of the bottle, but if the neck of the bottle is too narrow or you don't want to contaminate it, pour a small amount of ink into a shallow plastic or Styrofoam cup (without wax) or other nonfood dish you can discard or easily wash. You'll want a separate shallow cup for each ink that you use.

- If you're using watercolor paper rather than heavy cardstock, measure the watercolor paper and cut it to the size of card desired. Or you can keep it flat and cut out the card after you finish your ink print but before you attach the seashells.

- Make a large rectangle with deep blue ink on the face of the heavy cardstock or watercolor paper, using an artist's large paintbrush. Let the ink dry.

- Paint waves of deep blue and turquoise inks with a small round (#4 to #6) paintbrush. Let dry.

- Use hard-bonding glue on the seashells and adhere to the card. Let dry.

- Mail the finished card in a padded envelope.

Invitations

quick and easy • computer-assisted

If you're sending invitations for an event or party, you'll want to make a card that will impress the recipient. Work with a theme if you can.

You can work with type in Microsoft Word, Quark XPress, Adobe InDesign, and other word document or layout programs as well as in Photoshop or other computer photo options, if you've installed the software. Of course, the more sophisticated you are at using a computer, the less help you'll need here.

MATERIALS

cardstock base

two-sided tape or glue stick

deckle scissors

clip art

computer

computer printer

paper for computer printout

● Choose a cardstock base that will enhance the colors in the clip art.

● Cut out the clip art using deckle scissors. Adhere the clip art to the card face with a glue stick or two-sided tape.

● In your computer, choose a good, readable type font and point size. Write the what, where, when, and other details for your invitation. Print out the text on the desired paper.

● Cut out the text printout with deckle scissors.

● With two-sided tape or a glue stick, adhere the text to the inside of the card.

BOOKMARK INVITATION
computer-aided • gift

How about having an invitation with a surprise inside? This invitation to a book club has a bookmark attached to it. It's plain and simple.

If you're really savvy at using your computer, you won't need help here.

You Are Invited....

MATERIALS

raffia

cardstock base

cardstock for bookmark

clip art

hole punch

computer

computer font library (optional)

computer printer

- Use a cardstock that your computer printer will accept to create a bookmark that also acts as an invitation.

- Create the invitation text on computer, using an attractive type font in an appropriate size.

- Try out a few different colors that coordinate with the cardstock. Some, like yellow or pale colors, can be hard to read, and reds can be jarring. Dark blues and dark greens usually work nicely.

- Don't mix too many fonts on a single card; the result can be chaotic and difficult to read.

- Use clip art to support your theme. In this case, the invitation is for a book club; members will be reading a book about the Adirondacks.

- Make two holes in the card face, near the top, and string raffia through it. Attach the bookmark to the cover of the card with the raffia, either tied behind on the inside of the card or into a nice bow on the front of the card.

HINT: You can also make a regular invitation with all details inside the card and attach a bookmark to the card face.

Jewelry

CHARM FOR BRACELET
average complexity

Jewelry, even inexpensive costume jewelry, can make a nice gift when attached to a greeting card. Depending on the baubles and beads, it can make a dazzling card presentation. Use decorative papers and a little foil or metallic ribbon to enhance shiny, glittery jewelry.

MATERIALS
2 colors of corrugated cardstock
plain cardstock base
Mylar stars on tiny metallic string
thin wire
thin nail (for punching a hole)
rubber cement
clear package tape
charm (or other small piece of jewelry)

- Set aside the cardstock base.

- Cut a piece of corrugated cardstock to fit the front of the card on the plain cardstock base.

- Tear by hand a second piece of corrugated cardstock of a different color to make irregular edges. This will be a decorative base that will also reveal the first layer of corrugated cardstock.

- Generously use rubber cement on the front of the first corrugated cardstock where you plan to place the second torn piece of corrugated cardstock. Then generously use rubber cement on the bottom of the second, torn corrugated cardstock. Let both dry. This is called dry mounting.

- After the rubber cement is dry (in about 30 minutes), carefully position the top corrugated cardstock on the bottom corrugated cardstock. In the photo, you'll see that the grain on the bottom cardstock was positioned vertically while the grain for the second, torn corrugated cardstock piece was horizontal. Be careful. After the two glue-covered surfaces meet, they cannot be removed.

- Punch two tiny holes through the front of the card near the middle. I used a thin nail to make the hole, but other found tools, like a pushpin, could do the trick.

- Pull a thin wire through the holes and twist it around the small ring on the charm (normally used for attaching it to the bracelet). Make the twist on the back side of the charm; this will help secure the charm to the cardstock.

- Wrap the Mylar stars or other adornment around the entire card and secure them to the back with package tape.

- Using the dry-mount method, apply rubber cement to the front of the plain cardstock and the back of the corrugated paper you have already assembled. Let dry.

- Carefully place the two pieces together. When they've bonded, they cannot be pulled apart. You'll be able to hide your work.

- Mail the finished card in a padded envelope.

WITH THIS RING
quick and easy

When my husband proposed to me, he created a card of several pages. Inside he wrote a poem. On the front of the card, he tied an engagement ring with a ribbon. Even if you cannot write a poem or other little ditty, you can make a lovely card.

MATERIALS

colored cardstock base

colored paper

foil paper

decorative paper

deckle scissors

two-sided tape or glue stick

ribbon

ring (costume or fancy)

● Use a colored cardstock base.

● With deckle scissors, cut a square or rectangle of contrasting-color paper smaller than the card face. Adhere the paper to the front of the card with two-sided tape or a glue stick.

● Cut a narrow band of foil paper with deckle scissors. Adhere the narrow band to the card with two-sided tape or glue stick.

● Cut out decorative paper (last layer) with deckle scissors into a square or rectangle shape. Place this paper on top of the band, carefully centering it. After deciding where you want it, use two-sided tape or a glue stick to adhere it to the paper(s) on the card face.

● Punch two small holes in the card with a thin nail. Thread a ribbon through the holes and tie a ring on the card. Finish with a bow in the front of the card that secures the ring. On the reverse side (verso) of the card face, tape the back of the ribbon to ensure that it stays in place.

● Mail the finished card in a padded envelope, or, better yet (especially if it's precious), deliver it in person.

HINT: A whimsical piece of jingly jewelry could be nifty for a daughter, granddaughter, or niece's gift. Adjust the formality of the card to suit the recipient. Choosing the right decorative paper will make a difference.

Keepsakes

KEEPSAKE WITH CHILDREN'S ARTWORK
quick and easy • recycle • kid-friendly

The kitchen refrigerator may be the gallery for your children's art, but what do you do when you take the artworks down? You could recycle the art to make a card and send it to grandma and grandpa.

Here's a nice rainy-day project for children. Precut white or any color of drawing paper to a size that would fit on a standard card face. Then let children begin drawing or painting with their favorite tools.

MATERIALS

child's artwork
cardstock base
scissors
two-sided tape
embellishments (optional)

● Using ready-made cardstock is a fast way to make this card.

● Adhere the child's artwork to the card with two-sided tape.

● Each finished card will have its own personality.

HINT: For more fun, let the children use glitter, sequins, and other embellishments.

KEEPSAKE OF EVENT
quick and easy

Remember that wonderful evening you had going out with your favorite friend? Make a keepsake card as a thank-you to send to your friend with memorabilia that suggests the tone of the event and the evening. The card in the photo helps me remember a night at the theater that I shared with a friend.

MATERIALS

cardstock larger than the postcard

postcard (home or away)

ticket

restaurant clipping

decal

theatre program clippings

two-sided tape

deckle scissors

- Begin with a cardstock that's slightly larger than the local postcard. It will serve as a sort of frame.

- With two-sided tape, adhere the postcard to the front of the cardstock.

- Cut up the program that came with the play. Use photos from the play, your ticket stub(s), an ad from the restaurant where you ate, and some decals or other memorabilia. Affix each item to the card with two-sided tape.

KEEPSAKE WITH OLD PHOTOS
average complexity

Enjoy old black-and-white photos with this keepsake card.

MATERIALS

corrugated or plain cardstock base

decorative or solid-colored paper

old B&W photos

deckle scissors

two-sided tape

packaging tape

handwritten or computer text

raffia

- Begin with a cardstock base.

- With deckle scissors, cut decorative or solid-colored paper slightly smaller than the card face. Adhere the decorative paper to the cardstock with two-sided tape.

- Also with two-sided tape, mount the photos on the decorative paper.

- Add any text you desire with another slip of paper. A computer printout in a fancy font on nice paper would work, or use your best handwriting. You can deckle-cut the edges so that your caption fits below the photos.

- Wrap the card with raffia and tie a small corner bow.

- On the back of the card, use packaging tape to secure the raffia.

Grandma & Grandpa in 1951

Lace

LACE DOILY
quick and easy • feminine

When you're in a hurry but want to send a friend a feminine card, try this trick with a lace doily and an appliqué. To please an avid gardener, you could find a butterfly and flower appliqué. Naturally, all kinds of appliqués could work, depending on the theme you want to establish.

MATERIALS

cardstock base

doily

two-sided tape

deckle scissors

appliqué

- Select a pretty card base. Ready-made cardstock will be quickest.

- On the front of the card, affix a small doily with two-sided tape.

- Cover the center of the doily with an appliqué.

- For a little extra decoration, cut two or three sides of the cardstock with deckle scissors.

LACE FABRIC
feminine

Find a small piece of real lace, perhaps a scrap from a sewing project. Or you could buy a bit of lace from a fabric store. If you can sew, you'll enjoy making this card. If the recipient sews, too, that's all the better.

MATERIALS

white or light-colored cardstock base

long, solid-colored piece of cardstock

deckle scissors

fabric lace

sewing scissors

two-sided tape

brads

die-cut flowers

● Use a ready-made white or light-colored cardstock base or make your own; set it aside.

● With deckle scissors, cut a long piece of colored cardstock so that it's 1.5 times the length of the front of the card. Fold in each end of the colored cardstock so that its total size, with both ends folded in, will be a little less than that of the front of the card. (See the folded finished lavender example in the photo which also reveals a white border, the base cardstock.)

● With deckle scissors, cut the end flaps to a decorative V-shaped point.

- Trim a piece of lace to fit inside the folded cardstock, and adhere with two-sided tape to the colored cardstock.

- Then put two-sided tape on the inside of the V-shaped flaps and seal the flap to the lace.

- Using a die-cut flower shape and a metal decorative brad, punch a hole with the brad through the layers of colored (lavender shown here) cardstock and lace and fasten the brad. Our example uses two flowers and two brads, one for each flower.

- Finally, with two-sided tape, affix the assembled colored cardstock with lace, die-cut flowers, and brads to the light-colored cardstock base you had set aside. It will act as a sort of frame for the rest and show off the deckle-cut border of the folded color cardstock.

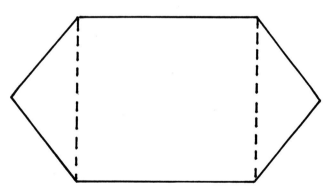

Fold along dotted lines.

LACE TRIM
feminine

A little lace makes cards feminine and fancy, while
reminding us of romantic
valentines, little girl charms,
doting grandmothers, summer
nightgowns, and tea time.

Dress up a card with lace
for a female friend or relative
who needs a pick-me-up.

MATERIALS

ready-made decorative
cardstock

decorative papers

two-sided tape

deckle scissors

lace trim or lace ribbon

packaging tape

sewing scissors

● Begin with a pretty, decorative cardstock base. With sewing scissors
or ordinary scissors, cut one or two short strips of lace trim to fit
the front of the card with a little extra extending on the reverse side.
To secure the lace trim, use packaging tape on the reverse (verso)
side of the card face.

● For the card in the photo, I used ³/₄-inch (2-cm) lace ribbon that's
about 8 inches (20 cm) long on a card base that's 4¹/₂ x 6 inches
(11.5 x 15.24 cm).

● Over the lace, add a square of decorative paper cut with deckle
scissors. Two-sided tape works nicely to attach the decorative paper
square on top of the lace.

● As a final touch, on top of the decorative paper, place a decorative
motif. Attach it with two-sided tape.

● If you want to hide your work (the taped lace), attach a sheet of
decorative paper with two-sided tape on the back (verso) of the
"front cover" of the card.

Magnets

ART OR TEXT MAGNET

quick and easy • computer-aided

This project is so simple that you could probably do it blindfolded. Use a small art print or recycle a greeting card.

The magnet, about the size of a business card, comes in small packages and can be found in office supply stores.

MATERIALS

cardstock base

art or computer text

scissors

business-card-size magnet with adhesive back

two-sided tape

- On your computer, create rows of text with the word(s) or phrases that suit the occasion.

- Alternate each row with different colors of text. If you have a PC and use Microsoft Word, highlight a row of text with your cursor, then go to the Format menu, scroll down to Font, then in the Font dialogue box change the color under Font Color. You can do this with every other word, every other phrase, or every other line of text, as you wish. Try out a pattern that suits you.

- You could also work with layout software that allows more manipulation of color backgrounds, such as Quark XPress or Adobe InDesign. You'll also have box border and color selection options in those or other computer layout software programs.

- Adhere the "Hello" or other message card tag to the magnet.

- Fasten the magnet to the cardstock base with two-sided tape.

- If you have a Mac, some of the newer models allow you to manipulate type and layout designs as you wish. It's also possible to do this in Adobe Photoshop or in Adobe Illustrator programs, but if you're savvy about those programs, you won't need help here.

- You'll be able to do fancy things like wrapping text or creating calligrams (shapes like apples or hearts made out of calligraphy) or doing other interesting things.

HINT: For fancy borders, you could simply use deckle scissors instead of trying to fashion something in your computer layout program. Colored paper for the printout also will serve instead of a color box generated by a computer program.

ART VARIATION

- Use ready-made cardstock. If you choose one with embossed borders, the finished look will be more decorative.

- Trim a print of the desired artwork to the size of the magnet. Peel off the paper backing to reveal the sticky side.

- Carefully position the art on the magnet.

- With two-sided tape, press the art print and magnet into the front of the card.

PUPPY MAGNET
quick and easy • gift

How cute is this little puppy magnet attached to the card? It's surely cute enough for the recipient to use on the refrigerator door. Of course, you'll want to find a magnet that suits the person receiving your card. You'll want to choose a magnet that isn't too heavy so that it stays adhered to the card.

MATERIALS

cardstock base

decorative paper

small refrigerator magnet

two-sided tape

deckle scissors

- Cut out decorative paper with deckle scissors and adhere the decorative paper to the cardstock base with two-sided tape.
- Affix the magnet to the decorative paper with two-sided tape.
- Mail the card in a padded envelope.

Mesh
quick and easy • *textured*

Dress up paper and stickers with an overlay of mesh in a desired color. You'll find mesh in arts and crafts stores in various colors.

MATERIALS

cardstock base

colored paper

stickers

mesh

scissors or paper cutter

two-sided tape

- Begin with ready-made cardstock base if you're in a hurry.
- Cut colored paper slightly smaller than the front of the card.
- Attach stickers here and there around the colored paper in the desired design. I've used a "Thinking of You" greeting as well.
- Cut mesh to the size of the card face.
- With two-sided tape, affix the mesh over the stickers and any message to the card near the edges of the card face.

Nature's Elements

AUTUMN-LEAVES PAPER PRINTS
quick and easy • multiple cards

In the fall, collect beautiful leaves found on sidewalks and paths. Immediately take these freshly fallen leaves to a photocopy store to make laser color copies. Play with variations by reducing the size, changing the arrangement, or trying out colored paper (whether for the background or the printouts). What results is your own decorative paper for card-making.

MATERIALS

colorful fall leaves

color laser-print photocopier

laser photocopy paper

scissors or paper cutter

cardstock base

two-sided tape or glue stick

deckle scissors (optional)

ribbon or decals (optional)

● Gather freshly fallen, brilliantly colored autumn leaves. You'll want fairly clean, disease-free leaves. (You may want to rinse and carefully dry them on paper towels as necessary. But the less you handle them, the better.) Smaller leaves work best for displaying a pattern of multiple leaves.

● Arrange the leaves face down on a clean color laser-print photocopier bed. Place a sheet of colored or plain paper behind the leaves; it will become the background color. Make a test copy. Try reducing the leaves to 50% or even to 25%. Make another test copy. Rearrange the leaves if you're not satisfied. Change the size of the photocopy to suit your aesthetic sensibilities. Remember that you can in turn reduce a photocopy of a photocopy if you want a very small pattern of leaves.

● If you're in a hurry, use a ready-made cardstock, or make your own. Cut out the photocopy of fall leaves so that it is slightly smaller than the card face.

- Bond the decorative-leaves photocopy with two-sided tape or a glue stick to the card face.

- Embellish as desired with deckle scissors, ribbon, text, or decals. Since nature has its own grace, you may not want to do anything more than display this elegant leafy print.

HINT: Placing the colored sheet background on top of the leaves will help protect the photocopier's lid from any dirt. When finished, clean the photocopy bed with alcohol and a soft cloth or consult the photocopy store attendant for the proper cleaning procedure. (He will probably prefer to do this himself.) Avoid using leaves that might leave a sappy mark.

The photocopy-shop attendant might scream foul, but the leaves won't damage the machine. Clean the photocopy bed properly and avoid using any diseased leaves or scratchy twigs.

BIRCH-BARK PRINT
rustic • masculine

When walking in the woods you may find some wonderful peelings of birch tree bark and some twigs. Strip the thin bark from your own tree and make a color laser photocopy. Making cards from the actual bark is not easy because the bark curls and is difficult to flatten.

An artist friend paints birds directly on birch bark.

You can fashion your own postcard if you have access to white birch bark, but meanwhile here's a card facsimile.

MATERIALS

cardstock base

photocopy of birch bark (or another bark)

paper cutter

solid-colored cardstock

two-sided tape

hard-bonding glue

twigs

hole punch

raffia

scissors

- Make a color laser photocopy of white paper-birch bark.

- Trim the birch-bark photocopy so that it's slightly smaller than the card face. A paper cutter can do this job neatly. Adhere the birch-bark photocopy to the cardstock base with two-sided tape.

- Cut a narrow strip of contrasting cardstock and center it on the card vertically. Adhere the strip to the face of the card with two-sided tape.

- Measure and trim the twigs to the length of the card. Ideally, the twigs should be as flat as possible.

- Lay the twigs on the contrasting strip in the center of the card and pour a few drops of hard-bonding glue in the center. Let dry.

- After the glue is dry and hard, you can gently work with embellishments.

- Punch a hole on both sides of the stack of twigs. You'll want each hole placed very close to the twigs.

- Thread the raffia through the holes and tie a knot in front of the card. With scissors, trim off the excess raffia.

- Mail the finished card in a padded envelope.

FEATHERS
quick and easy

Peacock feathers (you'll need just one) add whimsy and beauty to a card. You could use feathers from other birds, but the peacock feather easily does the trick. If you don't have access to lovely bird feathers, you could also buy feathers at an arts and crafts store.

MATERIALS

cardstock base

peacock tail feather (or other beautiful feather)

two-sided tape

vellum

- Since the "eyes" of peacock tail feathers are very large, you'll need to make a large card with cardstock.

- Using two-sided tape, adhere the tape to the "eye" of the feather. Press down the tape and attached feather onto the cardstock.

- Cover the front and back of the cardstock with vellum, cut to size.

- Use a strip of two-sided tape on the back of the cardstock to adhere the vellum to the cardstock.

LEAF PRINT
average complexity

Find a freshly fallen leaf or several leaves to create the motif for your card. All kinds of leaves will work nicely: maples, oaks, sycamores, ginkgos, rose leaves, or ferns. Just make sure that the leaf isn't too dry or brittle. You could detach a fresh leaf from its tree or plant, say, when preparing cut roses for a vase.

You'll want to capture with your print not just the outline of the leaf but its vein structure. Experiment with different kinds of leaves and different colors of ink pads.

MATERIALS

one or more leaves

large ink pad

rubber gloves (optional)

photocopy paper or other thin paper

solid colored paper

cardstock base

deckle scissors

decorative papers

two-sided tape

Press the leaf into the ink pad.

Rubbing leaf-impression onto paper with a spoon.

● Press a leaf into a large ink pad. (I've used just one for the card shown.) Rubber gloves will protect your fingers.

- Quickly and carefully position the inked leaf ink-side-down on the colored paper.

- Place a thin sheet of photocopy or other paper on top of the leaf. Rub the top sheet of paper with the curved side of a spoon.

- Carefully lift the top sheet of paper and leaf from the colored paper. You should have an inky image of the leaf with all the veins impressed on the colored paper. You can repeat this process with more leaves if you wish.

- With deckle scissors, cut out the colored paper with its leafy impression(s).

- Cut out a larger square of decorative paper using deckle scissors. Another square or rectangle of decorative paper can be used for the card face. Use deckle scissors if you wish for this bottom layer.

- Stack each layer of paper, with the leaf print on top. Adhere them together with two-sided tape in between.

- For interest, you could arrange your papers slightly askew.

Onion Prints

handmade paper • average complexity

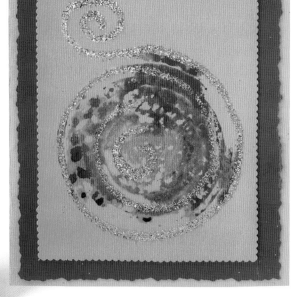

Please don't cry! We'll be using a Vidalia onion to make great paper. Onions make wonderful prints and designs. If you want to enhance the design, you can add glitter or other embellishments.

MATERIALS

colored cardstock base

onion

kitchen paring knife

white or colored paper or cardstock

watercolor paint

small artist's paintbrush

glitter (optional)

two-sided tape or glue stick

glue pen

deckle scissors (optional)

scissors or paper cutter

- Cut an onion down the middle. You can cut the onion from tip to tip or from side to side, whatever you wish. Each pattern will be different.

- Cut out a sheet of white or solid-color paper or cardstock. Use deckle scissors, regular scissors, or a paper cutter.

- With watercolor paint and an artist's paintbrush, brush different colors on the cut face of the onion.

● Firmly press the painted side of the onion face down on the solid-color paper. Carefully lift the onion to reveal the impression. You'll have an onion print that bears the individual onion's many rings.

● Let the print dry.

● If desired, embellish the onion print with glitter by first drawing a design with a glue pen. Then quickly sprinkle the glitter over the glue and let it dry a few moments.

● With a glue stick or two-sided tape, adhere the onion-print cardstock to the face of the colored cardstock base.

● For more interest, use more decorative or colored paper layers.

HINT: If you use glitter, shake off the excess glitter onto a piece of paper, fold the paper, and funnel the glitter back into the bottle. Save your glitter for other projects.

Ornaments

METAL ORNAMENT
quick and easy • gift • holiday

At Christmas, you could send a Christmas card that includes a simple gift ornament. The idea is to remove the ornament from the card and hang it on the Christmas tree or perhaps in a child's room.

Ornaments are not only for Christmas. I'm sure you'll be able to dream up other occasions and find or create ornaments to suit them.

If you don't want to make your own, a metal ornament to suit the occasion can be found in most craft stores.

MATERIALS

metal ornament or handmade ornament

sheet of holiday decorative paper or wrapping paper

scissors or paper cutter

cardstock base

raffia or yarn

two-sided tape

hole punch

- Cut a sheet of holiday decorative paper or wrapping paper slightly smaller than the face of the card.

- Mount the holiday paper to the card with two-sided tape.

- Punch a hole through the top of the card.

- Thread raffia through the hole in the card and the ornament. Tie the raffia. The receiver can untie the raffia, remove the ornament, and hang it with the retied raffia on the Christmas tree or in a child's room.

- Mail the finished card in a padded envelope.

PAPER ORNAMENT
quick and easy • gift • recycled

If you'd like to recycle holiday cards, here's one suggestion. Make a paper handmade mitten or other ornament to hang on a tree or decorate a package.

If you can knit or crochet something tiny to attach to the card, you won't need our suggestions here.

MATERIALS

old holiday card(s)	yarn
scissors	sequins (optional)
cardstock base	two-sided tape
holiday decorative paper	hard-bond glue
paper cutter (optional)	rubber cement

- From an old holiday card, cut out the shape of winter mittens, both front and back. You'll be making a pair (or four pieces total when counting front and back for the mittens). Or make a single large mitten front and back.

- Apply rubber cement to the back side of all the mitten pieces and let them dry. This is a dry-mount method.

- While the glue dries on the mittens, cut out holiday wrapping paper or other decorative paper, slightly smaller than the card face. Tape the decorative paper to the card using two-sided tape.

- Stretch yarn across the top of both mittens when the rubber cement is dry. Keep the mittens fairly close to each other and allow a generous amount of extra yarn beyond each mitten so that you can tie a bow. If you plan ahead, you could make a sort of cuff for the mittens (cut them long, well beyond the wrist) that will hold the yarn just as loops in curtains allow you to hang them from curtain rods.

- Prepare to bond the two pieces (back and front) of the mittens together. This bonding will also help hold the yarn in place. Be careful where you place them, because after bonding the mittens will not separate.

- If you'd like to decorate the mittens, apply a little hard-bonding glue on the front of the mitts and affix sequins to them for added sparkle.

- Cut two small slits near the top of the card face about 1 inch (2.5 cm) apart. Or use a hole punch to make these holes.

- Slide the yarn through the slits and let the mittens hang down the front of the card.

- Tie a bow on the inside of the card. Your receiver will be able to remove and use the mittens ornament.

HINT: If you simply want to make one or more mittens or another ornament that is adhered to the card, you'll probably want to secure the yarn on the back of the card face (verso side) with tape. If you wish, cover the back of the card with decorative paper. Use two-sided tape between that layer and the cardstock.

Outrageous Collection

pizzazz • recycled

Just as you might prepare a feast from refrigerator leftovers, you can create a card from the collection of leftovers in your craft box.

Don't forget items you didn't know what to do with, like netting from supermarket fruit boxes or misplaced buttons. Colors do not have to match. The more outrageous your creation, the more fun the card will be.

This supply list includes what I used to make this card. Gather materials from found objects around your house; they'll dictate how to assemble the individual card.

MATERIALS

cardstock base

(leopard print and zebra print) decorative paper(s)

feathers

star brads

button(s)

silk flowers

sticker(s)

netting

hard-bonding glue

two-sided tape

one-sided tape

- Gather your own collection and create your own card. Here's how I put my concoction of disparate materials together.

- With two-sided tape, I adhered the leopard print to the cardstock base, leaving a little of the cardstock revealed on top.

- I folded a piece of zebra print paper in half and affixed it to the base of the card only with two-sided tape. The folded edge of the zebra paper was kept roughly in the middle of the card.

- I fastened two star brads to the card's two bottom corners.

- I placed a sticker on top of the zebra print. Then I gathered the netting, feathers, and silk flowers and taped them with one-sided tape under the zebra print. To finish off the pocket, I closed up the sides of the zebra paper with two-sided tape.

- I fastened another star brad to the upper end of the card.

- With a dab of hard-bonding glue, I secured the button to the corner of the card.

- Mail the finished card in a padded envelope.

Oversized Cards

challenging

Send a magnificent huge card to that special person who needs to hear from you. Forget about those tiny note cards that you can barely fit enough words on. This card will let you ramble on with lots of things to say. Or write large for someone who has difficulty reading small print. Kids also like them.

Oversized cardstock can be found in photocopy shops, office supply stores, or arts and crafts stores.

MATERIALS

oversized cardstock	cutting mat
floral decorative paper	craft knife
striped decorative paper	stickers (optional)
glue stick	deckle scissors

- The pink cardstock base is 11 x 17 inches (28 x 43 cm). Score and fold it in half. On a paper cutter, trim to 8 x 10 inches (20 x 25 cm).

- The decorative paper has a pink stripe and coordinates with the floral decorative paper we'll use in the next step. Cut out the striped paper with a paper cutter about 1/3 inch (0.8 cm) shorter than the cardstock cover on all four sides. Adhere the decorative striped paper to the face of the cardstock with a glue stick.

- The large floral decorative paper has flowers that connect to each other. Trim it to fit the card cover on top of the coordinating striped paper. Use deckle scissors to make the edge more interesting.

- Things get a little challenging now. You'll need to decide what flowers to cut around to form a loose border. You'll need to cut around all four sides and then remove the middle that's cut out. Use your craft knife and carefully cut around the flowers on a cutting mat to protect your table.

- When you remove areas in the middle and around the flower shapes, you'll reveal the striped decorative paper beneath. Position the cutout in a desirable way over the striped paper. If it looks good, adhere the large floral border to the card with a glue stick.

- For the design shown, cut out a flower from the leftover paper and glue it in the middle of the striped paper. Also glue stickers of smaller flowers randomly on the striped paper.

Wishing
You
A Great
Trip

Paper Designs

BLACK-AND-WHITE PAPER
elegant • sophisticated

If you make your own hand-made paper, no one will have anything quite like it. Then you can really say about your card, "I made it myself!" We also work with other paper design styles here.

Also find directions for other paper designs: Splatter Prints (p.131), Sponge Prints (p. 132), and Squeegee Prints (p. 134).

MATERIALS
white cardstock base

black paper

hole punch

two-sided tape

handmade squeegee-painted paper

gossamer ribbon

deckle scissors (optional)

- Begin with a white cardstock base.

- Cut a piece of black paper slightly smaller than the front of the card. (You'll find black paper in most arts and crafts stores, often in the scrapbook section.)

- Use two-sided tape or a glue stick to adhere the black paper onto the front of the card. For added interest, place it slightly askew.

- Make textured paper using the squeegee method (see p. 134) and white and black acrylic ink.

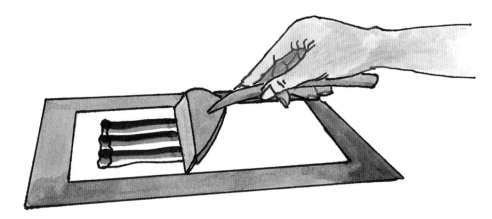

Using a squeegee to pull paint across paper.

- Cut the squeegee-painted paper slightly smaller than the black paper and adhere it to the black paper on the card face with two-sided tape. Set it askew in a direction opposite to that of the black paper.

- With a hole punch, punch two holes into the card face. To maintain the skewed theme, punch them on opposite sides.

- Thread a gossamer ribbon through the holes and tie a bow on the front of the card.

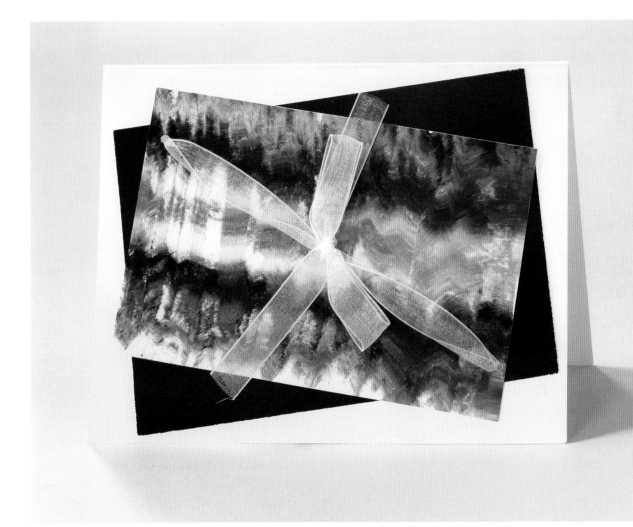

CRACKLE PAPER
time-consuming • rustic • masculine

If you're after a rustic look, this is it. The distressed appearance of old peeling paint has become very appealing today in antique or faux antique home furnishings and decorating. It also works well as the background or foreground for more masculine card designs.

Making crackle paper isn't difficult. It simply requires adequate drying time between each stage, so you'll want to plan a little ahead.

MATERIALS

two-ply Bristol drawing paper

acrylic paint (two colors)

crackle compound

wide sponge brush

wide, coarse brush

- With a wide sponge brush, brush acrylic paint on a sheet of heavy drawing paper. I've used dark gray paint for the first step shown here. Let the paint dry.

- Then brush on crackle compound with a wide, coarse brush. Allow the crackle compound to dry.

- With a wide sponge brush, brush on a second color of acrylic paint. We used off-white as shown in the photo. Let the acrylic paint dry.

- The finished crackle paper will make a nice card. Perhaps you'll want to attach a message or leave it plain, adhere a "found art object," or otherwise create a card to suit the receiver.

PLASTIC-WRAP PAINTED PAPER
painted texture

Although this technique is similar to that of bubble-wrap handmade paper, the textured effect is somewhat different.

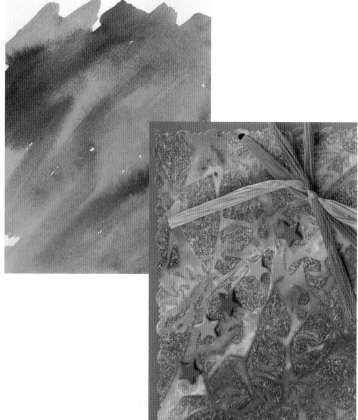

MATERIALS

heavy drawing paper

watercolor paint

artist's flat paintbrush
(1 to 2 inches wide)

water

plastic wrap or plastic bag

HINT: If you're afraid that you'll get paint on the book or other heavy object, put it inside a large freezer-type zipped plastic bag.

● With an artist's wide, flat paintbrush, mix watercolor paint with a little water and quickly brush the paint randomly on the heavy drawing paper.

● Change colors and repeat the process as many times as you wish. But avoid mixing too many colors in one spot since the effect will be muddy.

● While the paint is wet, quickly cover the paint with crumpled plastic wrap or a thin plastic bag. Press down into the paint. Put a heavy object, such as a book, over the plastic to secure it in place and to help create the impression on the paper.

● Let the paint dry a few hours or overnight.

● Remove the book or heavy object and the crumpled plastic wrap.

● If the paper is still damp, allow the paper to dry before using it.

SALT-PRINT PAPER
quick and easy • fun

This decorative paper is simple to make. You also don't have to go far from the kitchen.

MATERIALS

kosher salt

flat cardstock

ink or watercolor paint

- Set a sheet of cardstock on your worktable. Working very quickly, spread liquid ink or watercolor paint onto the cardstock with a paintbrush. Do not let the ink or paint dry.

- While it's still wet, sprinkle a little kosher salt on the wet ink or paint.

- Let dry.

- After the ink or paint is dry, you can brush the salt off the paper.

- Little crystallized spots are left. If you did not get these spots, you probably let the ink or paint dry too much before applying the salt.

- Use this salt-paper decorative cardstock to make a card. You can also cut it into desired shapes and adhere it to another cardstock base.

HINT: Protect the work table with newspapers or plastic before beginning. Ink or watercolor stains can be permanent.

WOOD-TEXTURE PAPER
quick and easy • masculine • rustic

This textured paper has a rugged look that men or woodworkers will appreciate.
   Instead of using carbon paper, you could do a rubbing on photocopy paper using a flat, broad crayon in a wood color like sienna on the surface with the raised-texture piece of wood underneath.

MATERIALS

photocopy paper

carbon paper

spoon

small piece of wood with full grain

HINT: As a next step, you can make a photocopy of this sheet to keep as a master copy. Make additional copies as you need them, using different colors of paper. Of course, you can also change the color of the wood texture on a color photocopier or with your own computer's photo software and a photo scanner.

● Use a small piece of wood with a full, raised grain. Weathered wood is best; painted or sanded wood will not work. It's advisable to use a weathered board that has been outdoors for a few years. Deck planks work well.

● Lay a sheet of photocopy paper (yes, the kind of inexpensive paper you'd normally use in a photocopier) directly on top of the wood.

● Place a sheet of carbon paper, face down, on top of the photocopy paper.

● On top of the two layers place a sheet of photocopy paper.

● Firmly holding down each layer, rub the curved side of a spoon on the top sheet of photocopy paper, going back and forth over the surface. Be sure to rub the entire length and width of the wood, covering as much of the paper as possible or as desired for your finished wood-grain paper.

● Remove the layers to reveal the bottom sheet of drawing paper with the pattern of the wood grain.

Photo-Mat Cards

quick and easy

Almost any well-composed photograph can make a nice card. Photos of children work nicely as gifts for doting grandparents and aunts and uncles. Naturally, your spouse or favorite relatives or friends are great, too. Create an interesting presentation by using embossed mats. You can find these mats at most arts and crafts stores or photo-supply stores.

MATERIALS

photograph

mat to fit

photo

one-sided

tape

cardstock base

scissors or paper cutter

two-sided tape

● Lay the mat (for photo or art) face down on the table. Place the photo face down on top of the back of the mat. With one-sided tape, tape the back of the photo to the back of the mat.

● Cut out cardstock slightly larger than the mat. With two-sided tape, join the cardstock to the mat. Then presto! You're done.

HINT: Many photo frames also come ready-made as cards. The mat essentially provides a frame, although the cardstock also does that as well.

Plastic-Wrap Prints

quick and easy • handmade paper

Under handmade plastic-wrap painted paper (see p. 109), review how to make decorative paper using plastic wrap to create a pattern with any color of inks or paints you choose. If you know that someone loves the color orange, for instance, you can make orange paper. Or you can create the appropriate colors to go with your theme.

MATERIALS

cardstock base	paper
brads (optional)	inks or watercolors
deckle scissors	decorative papers (optional)
raffia	two-sided tape
hole punch	
plastic wrap	

- Make handmade paper with various colors of paints or inks and plastic wrap to create a decorative pattern. Let it dry.

- With deckle scissors, cut the handmade paper slightly smaller than the face of the card. Adhere the paper to the card using two-sided tape.

OPTION: Cut other sheets of decorative papers to fit your desired design on the face of the card. Attach them with two-sided tape to the face of the card. Or randomly fasten decorative brads through the front of the card. Punch two holes in the card cover, thread raffia through the holes, and tie a bow. Mail the card in a padded envelope.

Pocket Card

quick and easy • gift

While we use a lottery ticket as a gift and theme here, you can create a pocket with your own little gift inside.

MATERIALS

cardstock base

new lottery ticket (gift)

2 lottery forms (for pocket and decoration)

brads

two-sided tape

scissors

Backside of card face

• This card uses a ready-made cardstock base.

• Make a pocket with a lottery form just the right size to hold the fresh lottery ticket. (Test the orientation, size, and shape first with a slip of paper or cardboard, if you wish.)

• Apply two-sided tape to three sides of the pocket and affix the pocket to the card base. Use decorative brads in the four corners of the pocket.

• Cut out other lottery forms to make the pocket more decorative and adhere them with two-sided tape.

• Slip the new gift lottery ticket in the pocket. Remember that it's time-sensitive.

OPTION: Make a pocket card out of other materials and present your enclosed flat, ticketlike gift.

Potato Prints

fun

It's easy to make your own imaginative stamp out of a potato.

MATERIALS

potato

cardstock base

kitchen or paring knife

craft knife

ink stamp pad(s)

ribbon, vellum, eraser-stamp embellishments (optional)

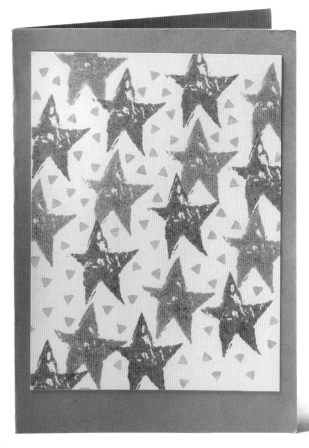

● To create a potato stamp, cut a potato in half with a kitchen knife.

● Using a craft knife, cut away the part of the potato you do not want as part of your design. Leave only the positive design as the print surface.

● Press the design (flat surface) on your potato stamp into the ink stamp pad and then firmly press it onto the cardstock.

● Return the stamp to the stamp pad and repeat the design as you wish on other spots on your card.

● Add embellishments like a ribbon or layer of vellum, or use a pencil eraser-stamp to dot the card as well.

HINT: Draw your design on the cut potato using a soft lead pencil if you think this will help you. Also try using different colors of ink stamp pads.

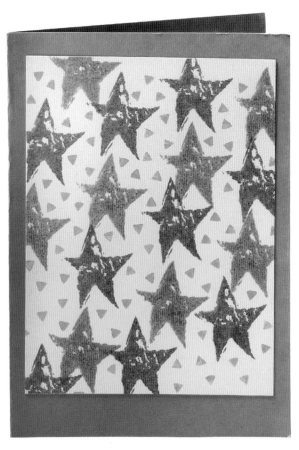

Potato print variations

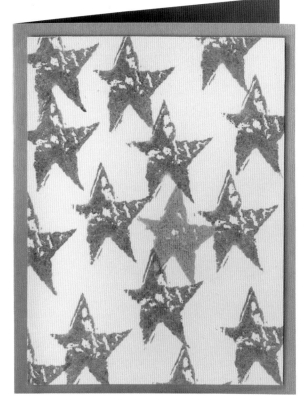

Quilling

challenging

Quilling is also known as paper rolling, paper scrolling, filigree, and mosaic. The term comes from the feather quill around which thin strips of paper were curled or rolled. Today various other implements are used for quilling.

Some versions of this craft are said to date from ancient China and Egypt. Since it depends on the availability of paper, it was more popularly practiced in Europe in the 1500s. Nuns and later proper young ladies learned the art. They often attached the quilling to the inside of a framed shadow box, and coordinated the backing with the quillwork displayed.

MATERIALS

cardstock base	glue
deckle scissors	decorative paper
quill paper or quill stickers	brads (optional)
	two-sided tape

- With deckle scissors, cut out decorative paper.

- Layer decorative paper in various sizes, as desired. Adhere the decorative papers to cardstock with two-sided tape.

- Glue on top of the decorative paper the quilled paper.

- Add brads or other embellishments if you wish.

- Mail the finished card in a padded envelope.

HINT: Today quill kits are available in craft stores or you can find quill decals. Many quillers use acid-free mat board instead of a shadow box. Find a recommended quill glue in an arts and crafts store.

Quilting Pins

average complexity • gift

Here's a special card to send to someone who sews quilts. Decorative papers with a calico design and decorative quilting pins make a wonderful card that's also a gift. The recipient can remove the quilting pins and use them. These pins look like flowers, so a flowerpot motif is just right.

MATERIALS

cardstock base

decorative paper

embossed cardstock

two-sided tape

quilting pins

- Cut out decorative paper to fit the cardstock base. If you can find a quilt print, that's best.

- Adhere it to the cardstock base with two-sided tape.

- Spread the pins in a fanlike design. The pins will be your bouquet of flowers.

- Affix the pins, at the pointed end, to the card with two-sided tape.

- Cut out embossed cardstock in the shape of a flowerpot.

- With two-sided tape, adhere the flowerpot on top of the base of the pins. Extra tape is good.

- Mail the finished card in a padded envelope.

Quilt-Paper Card

quick and easy • recycled

Here we use a variety of small printed decorative papers to create a popular quilt pattern called Around the World. You'll have fun creating your own paper quilt.

MATERIALS

decorative paper

scissors or paper cutter

cardstock base

two-sided tape

craft knife

ruler

- Cut decorative paper slightly smaller than the front of the card. On top of your cardstock base, adhere the decorative paper with two-sided tape.

- From two other decorative papers with different patterns, cut squares. For the card shown, cut three or four 1-inch (2.54-cm) squares from different decorative papers. You can cut your pieces to any size, as long as they're square.

- Beginning in the center of the card, adhere the first square to the middle of the card with two-sided tape.

- Using a different decorative patterned paper, affix four squares to each corner of the first square.

- On the top and bottom of the original square, fill in the gap with two other paper squares.

- If you make a larger card or a square card, continue adding squares.

Recycled Gift Tags & Holiday Cards

quick and easy • recycled

Recycling old holiday cards suggests all kinds of possibilities. You can use all or none of the materials below to create fresh new cards from old cards, tags, stickers, wrapping paper, ribbon, and the works. You can cut down large cards that still have white space inside for nifty gift tags or small cards.

POSSIBLE MATERIALS AND TOOLS

old cards

ready-made cardstock

wrapping paper

decorative paper

gift-tag stickers

photo border cards

scissors or paper cutter

deckle scissors (optional)

glue stick or two-sided tape

die-cuts

computer text

ribbon

brads

● Cards, tags, wrapping paper, even ribbon can be recycled to make new cards. A few cards shown in the photos consist of the front cut from an old card and adhered to a new cardstock base. You could also embellish gift tags and fasten them to new cardstock bases. To make still other cards, you can add your own computer-printout text in a fancy font on the face of the card. Some cards have ready-made borders, and you can make a frame for others. There's really no end to how creative you can be when recycling. Just have fun.

Ribbons

quick and easy

With your home computer and printer, decorative cardstock, and fabric ribbon, you can fashion a card quickly.

MATERIALS

decorative cardstock

computer with selection of fonts

computer printer

fabric ribbon

two-sided tape

scissors or paper cutter

deckle scissors (optional)

hole punch (optional)

- From your computer, choose a nice, decorative font and adjust the font size to fit your greeting on the face of the card. After you've played around with your greeting and are happy with it, print it out. Check the size against the face of the card with a little "white space" around it.

- Cut the text greeting to a size smaller than the card face. If your computer printer doesn't accept specialty paper, you can photocopy your greeting on the new paper and then cut it to the desired size.

- Trim and fold the cardstock.

- Cut a length of fabric ribbon to fit across or down the card. (Ours has a rose design.)

- With two-sided tape, adhere the ribbon to the card.

OPTIONS: Of course you can use ribbons in many ways. Use a hole punch to make holes in a card face so that you can thread the ribbon through it and tie it in front. Or use ribbon near the fold to make a booklet sort of binding.

Scherenschnitte

SCHERENSCHNITTE
(The Real Thing)
challenging

Scherenschnitte is the German term for paper cutting, an art found in many cultures. Designs can be highly complex or relatively simple.

To make your own scherenschnitte, you can use an X-acto knife or sharp scissors. Some people prefer to cut around a traced cutout pattern. Most prefer to create scherenschnitte on black paper, later attached to a light or contrasting background, because the black shape helps define the decorative cutwork.

MATERIALS

thin paper (preferably black)

craft knife (X-acto) or sharp scissors

spray adhesive

cardstock base

pencil

cutting mat

● Using thin paper and a pencil, lightly draw a design on the thin paper.

● With a cutting mat under the paper, use a sharp craft knife, such as an X-acto (size 11 blade works well, cut on the very tip only) to very carefully and gently cut out the design. Replace the X-acto blade as necessary when it gets dull.

● When you're finished cutting your design, cover the back of the design with spray adhesive. Be sure to do this in a well-ventilated area. Use a newspaper behind the design to avoid getting the adhesive glue all over.

● Gently lift the paper-cut design and carefully place it on the cardstock base.

● Press down on the design, taking care not to disturb it but ensuring that it adheres to the cardstock.

● Since scherenschnitte is so delicate, you may want to make a photocopy of the paper-cut art to create a card. Keep the "master" for more photocopy cards.

HINT: You can also make your own print from scherenschnitte. It won't have the three-dimensional quality of cut paper, but the effect is lovely.

SCHERENSCHNITTE MADE EASY

For an easy paper-cutting project, we can speed up the process with a few tools.

MATERIALS

cardstock base

thin paper

pencil

colored or decorative paper

hole punch

die-cut

deckle scissors

craft or X-acto knife

glue stick

● Begin with thin paper that's slightly larger than the card face. Fold the thin paper in half, taking care that when the design is unfolded (here we've used a heart), it will be oriented in the way you wish. With a pencil, draw the heart or another design (without the scallops) on one side of the folded thin paper. Remember that the fold should be in the middle of the design.

● Cut out the heart or other shape with deckle scissors.

● Using die-cuts and a hole punch, cut out the desired designs within the heart as you would when making a paper snowflake.

● *For the heart design*, carefully cut the design of the tulip on the edge of the fold with a craft knife. Remember that you are only cutting half the tulip. When you open the folded paper, the entire tulip will show.

● Affix the cut paper to the background paper with a glue stick.

● Cut the colored paper with deckle scissors.

● Adhere to the cardstock base with two-sided tape.

● *For the butterfly design,* fold the thin paper in half. Draw your half-butterfly design with a pencil on the folded paper. Use a craft knife, not scissors, to cut it out. Then draw "windows" in the butterfly's wings and use a craft knife to cut them out.

● Adhere the butterfly to colored cardstock or thick colored paper.

Screen Prints (Silkscreen)

challenging • multiple cards

Screen printing (silkscreen) offers exciting effects for making cards. It also enables you to make several cards of the same design. Many arts and crafts stores have screen-printing kits as well as mail-order catalogs. Since all of them vary somewhat from each other, it's best to follow the directions with the kit you purchase. However, to get an idea of the basics, follow these directions.

SCREEN-PRINTING KIT

emulsion and/or film

squeegee

ink

screen with fabric attached

OTHER MATERIALS

degreasing chemical

tape (for securing screens)

masking tape

sink with running water and a hose

heavy Bristol paper

work board (plywood or masonite)

- Design a motif, such as a photo silhouette, and print it in one or more colors. To print a few colors with a variegated appearance, you'll need dollops of a few colors.

- First degrease the screen and get ready to attach the image.

- Using a chemical process with a film stencil or photo-sensitive material, attach the desired design to the screen.

- Get ready to print the design. Lay down a sheet of heavy, smooth-finish Bristol paper (larger than your open-card design) on a work board. Tape all four corners to the work board with removable masking tape.

- Place the screen over the Bristol paper with the fabric facing the paper.

- On the top of the fabric area, not near the design, apply a few dollops of ink.

- Hold your squeegee firmly and run the rubber end of the squeegee through the ink and over your design. Just one swipe will do.

- Carefully lift the screen off, away from your paper. Your image will be there. Remove the masking tape and set the paper aside to dry, about an hour or so depending on climate.

⬦ Now use your squeegee to push the ink back to the top of the screen to be ready for the next printed card.

⬦ When you finish making multiple prints, you must clean the screen thoroughly with cold water from a hose. Do not let a full force of water hit the screen because it can remove or damage the image and screen.

⬦ After the ink dries, fold and trim the card to the desired size. Use a scoring tool and paper cutter for that job.

HINT: Protect your table, carpet, and furniture with plastic sheeting and wear a smock or old painting clothes.

Shaped Cards

fun • adults • teens and kids

Shaped cards can draw on many objects. Here are a few ideas for other shapes: butterfly, turtle, try-on beard with strings attached, snowman, sitting dog, purse, fish, sailboat, motorcycle, car, palm tree, bag with golf clubs, birthday cake, holiday ornament, pumpkin, mittens, heart, star, teddy bear, or outline of your home state, province, or country.

MATERIALS

cardstock base

scissors

craft knife

tracing paper

pencil

light box (optional)

two-sided tape

glue stick

decorative paper

deckle scissors

die-cuts

fine-point black marking pen

embellishments (optional)

- For all designs, make sure that the card's fold remains uncut and is either on the top or left side of the card. (You can take a decorative nick out of it, but you'll need to maintain the hinge.) For the mug, line up the handle with the fold.

- With a pencil, trace or draw the desired design onto tracing paper. Relatively flat shapes, like flip-flops, can be traced directly on the tracing paper.

- Go over the traced pencil lines with a fine-point black marking pen so that you can see the pattern through the cardstock, especially if the cardstock is a dark color.

- Using a light box or sunny window, trace the shape (mug, hat, or other) onto cardstock with a light pencil line.

- With scissors or a craft knife, use the pencil outline on the cardstock as a guide to cut out the desired shape. Depending on the cardstock's thickness, it may be easier to cut one layer at a time (first the front, then the back of the card). If you use a craft knife, be sure to protect your work table with cardboard or a cutting mat.

MUG

- Dress up the mug-shaped card with ink markers in various colors, and inside attach a packaged tea bag (or other surprise) with two-sided tape. If your friend is home on a bitter cold day, wouldn't this be a nice pick-me-up?

- To make sure the ink won't seep through to the message and vice versa, tape contrasting paper on the verso of the card face.

Silhouettes

keepsakes

Silhouettes are similar to scheren-schnitte in that you use cut paper. These silhouettes were popular in Colonial America. People and pets can be the models, seen in profile. Silhouettes are fun to shape, and they also make nice keepsakes.

You can create an earnest portrait or engage in caricature, depending on your wit, ability to whittle, and whimsy. Here we're creating more serious portraits. You can cut out simple black-on-white images or use decorative or colored papers behind them to enhance a desired theme.

MATERIALS

cardstock base

black construction paper

sharp scissors or craft knife

profile photo of subject

glue stick

two-sided tape

decorative paper

deckle scissors

pencil

- Using a photo of your subject's profile, trace the outline on black construction paper using a pencil.

- Cut out the silhouette with scissors or a craft knife.

- If you wish, cut out decorative paper with deckle scissors to use as background for the subject.

- Adhere the decorative paper to the cardstock with two-sided tape.

- If the pencil marks show and cannot be easily erased, place the reverse side of the silhouette face up. With a glue stick, affix the silhouette to the decorative paper.

Splatter Prints

quick and easy

Splatter prints

Sponge print (far right)

A few household items can create a dashing card. Don't throw away that old toothbrush; recycle it for this project. You'll want to wear a smock or apron or clothes you don't mind getting splattered with paint.

MATERIALS

cardstock

old toothbrush

watercolor paint

artist's paintbrush

household objects

dull, flat palette knife

- Using keys, lace, doily, leaves, and other household or garden items, place them on the cardstock.

- Wet the toothbrush with water and blot dry. This will soften the bristles.

- Work up some watercolor paint with water and an artist's paintbrush.

- Put newspaper behind the card to catch any excess paint splatter.

- Place the object(s) on the cardstock.

- Put paint on the toothbrush using the artist's paintbrush.

- Hold a palette knife in one hand. Rub the toothbrush on top of the knife, away from you, aiming toward the card. Warning: if you rub the toothbrush toward you, you will get splattered with paint.

- Let the paint dry a few minutes and remove your object.

- Add a greeting or use the card as is.

Sponge Prints

SPONGE-TEXTURE PAPER
quick and easy

Making a sponge texture on paper is about as easy as it gets. I prefer a natural sea sponge found in arts and crafts stores or bath shops. Paper and acrylic or watercolor paint are all you need to work with the sponge. Use one color or many colors; the creative process is up to you.

MATERIALS

cardstock or heavy drawing paper

paint (watercolor or acrylic)

natural sea sponge

water

plastic dish

artist's paintbrush

- Use a heavy cardstock or drawing paper. Colored cardstock is fine.

- With a small artist's paintbrush, mix a little paint in a plastic dish (the kind you can throw away). Mix in a little water if needed.

- Press the sea sponge into the paint you just mixed.

- Place the sponge on the paper. Move the sponge to a new spot. Add paint as needed.

HINT: You may want to wear plastic gloves to keep paint off your hands. Clean up with soap and water.

SPONGE-PRINT CARD

average complexity

Review the technique for sponge-texture paper on p. 132. You can create wonderful textures using one or many colors. Here we've used just one color.

MATERIALS

cardstock base

colored paper

pattern

sponge-texture paper

raffia

hole punch

two-sided tape

deckle scissors

- With deckle scissors cut a center circle in the card face (cardstock base).

- Cut the sponge-print paper to size for the card.

- With two-sided tape, affix the layers of decorative paper to the inside of the card so that it appears through the circular window created in the cardstock.

- Punch two holes in the card. Thread raffia through the holes and tie it.

Squeegee Prints

quick and easy

As you practice, this paper-making technique will allow you to create better and better squeegee prints that you can use as decorative paper or on their own for cards.

SQUEEGEE-TEXTURE PAPER

MATERIALS

acrylic paints (in its original plastic squeeze bottle)

heavy drawing paper

squeegee

- On a sheet of heavy drawing paper, squeeze paint from the acrylic paint squeeze bottle in a small lump on top of the paper. (Or drip a few small lumps from the bottle of acrylic paint.) Put several lumps in a line. Choose another color and squeeze it in next to the previous color.

- Add as many colors as you like.

Using a squeegee to pull paint across paper.

- Position your rubber-edge squeegee at the top of the paper, above the paint lumps. With pressure on the squeegee, run it down the length of the paper. You can pull the squeegee straight down or zigzag it from side to side as you pull the paint down. The design effect will be different depending on how you spread out the paint with the squeegee.

- Just one long sweep of the squeegee will do it. If you begin to mix the paint too much or have too many colors, the final print could become muddy.

- Let the paper dry completely before using it as a card base or as decorative paper.

SQUEEGEE-PRINT CARD

Squeegee-texture paper can be as fancy or as simple as you like. You select the colors and determine whether they'll be muted or dazzling.

MATERIALS

cardstock base

squeegee-texture paper

ribbon

text

two-sided tape

deckle scissors

- Cut out with regular or deckle scissors the squeegee-texture paper, making it slightly smaller than the front of the card.

- With two-sided tape adhere the squeegee-texture paper to the card.

- Tape a length of ribbon to the card.

- Cover the tape with a greeting. Attach the greeting with two-sided tape.

Stickers

quick and easy

If you have handy stickers or a nice print that you can cut apart to create your own stickers, you can craft a last-minute card.

MATERIALS

cardstock base

assorted stickers or color print(s)

scissors (optional)

rubber cement

● Begin with colorful cardstock base.

● From a larger color print or several prints, cut out the desired figures, images, or words. Arrange them on the face of the cardstock in the desired design. Use a dab of rubber cement on the back of the homemade stickers. Attach them to the card.

● When dry, rub off excess rubber cement.

Tags

allow extra time

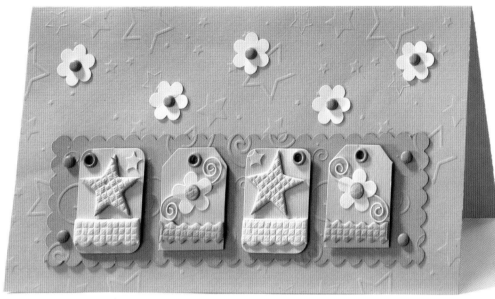

Making cards with tags can be simple or involved depending on how much time and creativity you use. One thing is for sure, you'll have fun.

NOTE: Tags are usually found in the paper crafting section of craft stores. They're also used in making scrapbooks.

MATERIALS

cardstock base

plain paper

flower die-cuts

colored or decorative paper

deckle scissors

tags

stickers (optional)

brads

two-sided tape

adhesive dots (optional)

- Cut flower shapes with a die-cut. Or if you wish, use packaged stickers from a craft or gift shop.

- With deckle scissors, cut colored paper into a rectangle. Attach the colored paper rectangle to the cardstock base with two-sided tape.

- Adhere the stickers and tags to the paper. Stickers will have adhesive. For tags, use two-sided tape.

- With brads, fasten the die-cut flowers to the cardstock and fasten the brads to the corners of the rectangle of colored paper.

- If you wish, cover your work on the reverse of the card face with colored paper cut to size and attached with two-sided tape.

- Mail the finished card in a padded envelope.

MORE TAGS

- Use a decorative card base.

- Cut out contrasting cardstock or decorative paper with deckle scissors.

- Add a decal or decorative paper to the tag, if you wish.

- Punch a hole in the card and thread raffia through the hole and tie it in a bow.

- Mail the finished card in a padded envelope.

Three-Dimensional Cards

quick and easy • fun

Who said that cards have to be flat? You can give dimension to your creation by the use of self-adhesive foam dots. They are available in craft stores and come with sticky glue on both sides. All you have to do is peel off the protective paper and press the sticky foam dots onto your card.

MATERIALS

firm cardstock base

decorative paper

heavy cardstock starfish or other appliqué

self-adhesive foam dots

deckle scissors

two-sided tape or glue stick

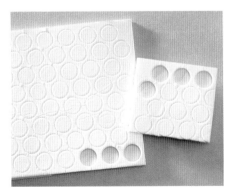

Adhesive foam dots.

● Begin with a firm cardstock base. Avoid very thin cardstock for these cards. Thicker ready-made cardstocks work better here.

● Cut a complementary decorative paper with deckle scissors as desired. Adhere the decorative paper to the cardstock with two-sided tape or a glue stick.

● The starfish shown is a heavy cardstock appliqué. Since the starfish is quite large, I used sticky dots in the middle of the body and on all points. Remove protective paper from one side of the sticky dot and adhere the sticky dot to the underside of the starfish.

● Remove the protective paper from the second side of the sticky dot and carefully place the starfish on the decorative paper. Press firmly on all sticky dots.

● Mail the finished card in a padded envelope.

Tie-dyes

fun • two-day project

Tie-dying is back in fashion on T-shirts. Did you know that you can tie-dye very easily at home with small scraps of fabric and a cup of ink or dye? It's very simple to make and you end up with wonderful results. Don't throw away those scraps of solid color or white cotton fabric from sewing projects.

MATERIALS

ink or fabric dye

plastic cup or jar (disposable)

cotton fabric

small rubber bands

cardstock base

pinking shears

iron

two-sided tape

aluminum foil

rubber gloves

large plastic spoon (disposable)

embellishments (optional)

TIE-DYED CIRCLE DESIGN

Pinch the center of the square cotton fabric scrap with your fingers and fold all the remaining fabric down, away from the area you're holding.

Pinch fabric for tie-dying.

● Using small rubber bands, wrap the first one near your center point at the tip of the fabric. Be sure to wrap this rubber band and each succeeding one as tightly as you can without breaking it

● About ¹/₂ inch (1.25 cm) from the first rubber-band wrap, wrap a second rubber band. Repeat this process until you are close to the end of the bundle.

● Pour a little ink or fabric dye into the cup, filling it about halfway.

● Wearing rubber gloves or using a large plastic spoon, submerge your bundle into the dye. Let it sit for about a half hour or the time given in the dye directions.

● With your rubber gloves or a large disposable plastic spoon, remove the bundle and place it on aluminum foil; set aside to dry. Allow a full day or more to dry.

- After the fabric is dry, carefully remove the rubber bands. If the fabric is still damp, let it air dry.

- Iron out the wrinkles. (You may want to protect your iron with another clean fabric on top of the tie-dyed fabric. Dye may leach onto the clean fabric.)

- Cut the tie-dyed fabric with pinking shears. Cut the cardstock to fit the tie-dye design. Use two-sided tape to fasten the tie-dyed fabric to the front of the card.

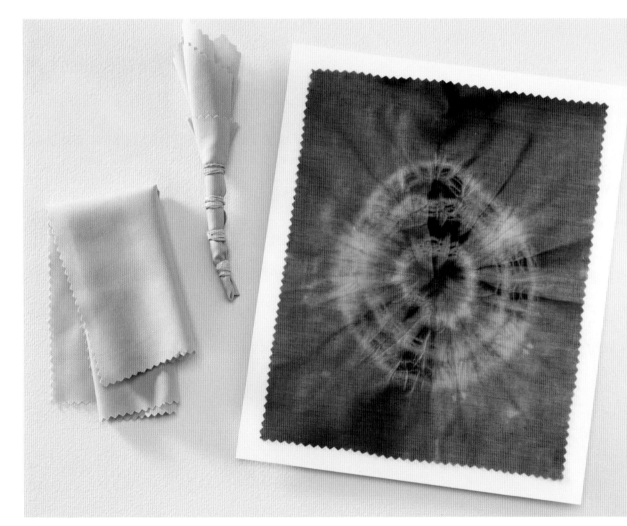

OPTION: Stitch or sew sequins or buttons to the card. To do that use a needle and thread and sew right through the front of the card. When finished, you can hide the thread on the inside of the card with decorative paper, attached with a glue stick or two-sided tape.

HINT: Save the dye in a glass or plastic jar with a tightly closed lid, and you can use it again. Waste not, want not.

TIE-DYED STRIPED DESIGN

● For a linear rather than a circular pattern, take the fabric and make accordion folds. About ¹/₂ to 1 inch (1.25 to 2.5 cm) folds work well.

● Using the rubber bands, wrap them around the entire bundle. Begin at one end and place the rubber bands about ¹/₂ inch to 1 inch (1.25 to 2.5 cm) apart.

● Follow the tie-dying procedure above for dipping, drying, and finishing.

● When you unfold the tie-dyed fabric, you'll have a striped design.

CAUTION: Ink or dye splashed on your clothes could be permanent. Wear a smock or apron to protect them. Also only use disposable tools for the tie-dying process.

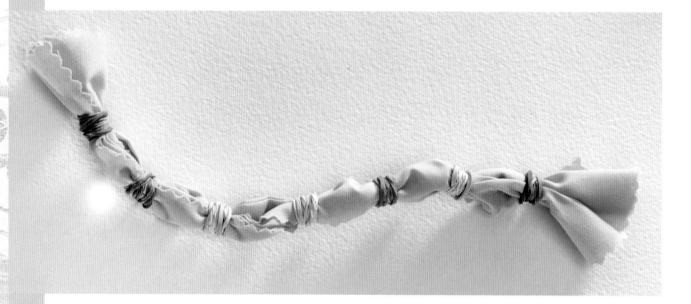

Tissue Paper

quick and easy

Tissue paper is thin and creates an interesting look when you can see the paper behind it. A satin ribbon with text adds a nice touch. This creates a card with texture.

MATERIALS

decorative cardstock

tissue paper

two-sided tape

ribbon decal

- Use a decorative cardstock base.

- Carefully tear tissue paper into the shape you want. Tearing a ragged edge adds more interest to the look.

- Affix the tissue paper to the card with two-sided tape.

- Mount a ribbon decal to the top of the tissue.

Useful Cards

quick and easy • practical

Follow various card-making techniques in this book and attach or glue something useful to the card, like a business card, calendar, or paper clips.

It's fun to make a card that the recipient can actually use. The challenge is to find useful things that are around the house.

Business card

Calendar card

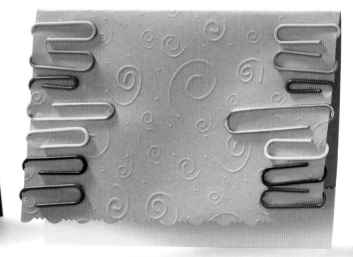

Paper-clip card

Vellum

QUICK VELLUM CARD
quick and easy • sophisticated

Adding a layer of vellum (a strong, cream-colored, see-through paper) to a card adds sophistication. Make a wedding invitation or another invitation to any event.

MATERIALS

white cardstock

decorative vellum

computer text

hole punch

ribbon

● Print out a greeting from your computer in a pleasing type font on white cardstock.

● Cut and fold the cardstock to the size of card you like.

● Cut and fold decorative vellum and slide it over the cardstock. You should have a front and back cover of vellum.

● Punch a hole through all four layers of vellum and card, near the edge of the fold.

● Thread a ribbon through the hole. Tie the ribbon in a bow.

VELLUM HOLIDAY CARD
quick and easy • sophisticated

We've used a pine-needle theme; you can substitute other patterns for other occasions.

MATERIALS

white cardstock base

two-sided tape

decorative paper

standard or deckle scissors

decorative printed vellum

raffia or ribbon

deckle scissors (optional)

hole punch

- Begin with a plain white cardstock base.

- Cut a strip of decorative paper to fit along one edge of the card; here I've used a pine-branch or a pine-needle print. You can cut the paper with standard or deckle scissors. Position the decorative paper on the cardstock and adhere the paper to the cardstock with two-sided tape.

- Use a pine-tree vellum print; cut and fold the vellum to fit the card.

- On the back of the card, use two-sided tape and bond the vellum to the cardstock. This will help prevent the vellum from shifting.

- Punch two holes through the cardstock, decorative paper, and vellum on the front of the card.

- Thread raffia or ribbon through the holes. Tie it in a bow on the front of the card.

Victorian Valentines & Other Fancies

BAROQUE VICTORIAN CARD
slightly challenging • feminine

The Victorians loved a highly decorated and embellished style in the various appointments of home interiors, a penchant which carried over to their elaborately detailed and ornate cards redundant with paper lace and multiple layered images.

MATERIALS

cardstock base

rhinestones

doilies

Victorian stickers

decorative paper

solid-colored paper

deckle scissors

two-sided tape

hard-bonding glue

adhesive dots

scissors

- Cover an entire cardstock base with decorative paper, such as a Victorian floral design. Use two-sided tape to adhere the paper to the card.

- Use a small round doily for the center medallion.

- With solid-colored paper and deckle-edge scissors, cut out the paper slightly larger than the doily. Trace a circle from a stencil. Or, if you're like me, you'll find a can, paper cup, or other round object to trace the circle.

- Affix a Victorian sticker (I've used a dog sitting in a teacup) to the center of the doily. Join the doily and solid paper with two-sided tape.

- Adhere the entire medallion to the card with adhesive dots. I used five on this card beneath the blue circle medallion. These "lifts" (what they were once called) give the card a very Victorian look.

- Cut a second round doily into quarters. Fasten the doily quarters to the corners of the card with two-sided tape.

- On each corner of the front of the card, fasten rhinestones on top of the doilies with hard-bonding glue.

- Mail the finished card in a padded envelope.

An alternative highly ornate Victorian card can consist of multiple stickers that create a design, like those of the dog in a tea cup or dancing cats shown on this page.

For a fussy, feminine appearance, you could also use a length of lace attached to the back of the card. Adhere the lace to the cardstock using two-sided tape. Cover the edges of the cut lace with decorative paper that's cut out with deckle scissors. (Also see lace card variations on pp. 82 to 85.)

VICTORIAN VALENTINES
quick and easy • feminine

During the Victorian age, many people created their own handmade cards with costly or artful embellishments, like hand-painted pictures, silk, lace, and other decorative items. What began in the English upper classes, perhaps with calling cards, soon spread to the middle class as card-making became increasingly popular in the 1860s for Valentine's Day and Christmastime. People spent hours making a single card.

Some wicked folks even sent vinegar valentines that anonymously delivered insults to someone rejected or disliked. Typically these cruel missives were delivered by the post office postage due, so the unwitting recipient even had to pay postage.

MATERIALS

cardstock base

stickers or decals

decorative paper

deckle scissors

two-sided tape

adhesive dots (optional)

lace

- Use ready-made cardstock to make this card quickly.

- Cut a square or rectangle with deckle scissors. Here we've made fancy corner cuts. Adhere the square or rectangle to the center of the card using two-sided tape.

- Affix a Victorian-style sticker to the square or rectangle.

- As an option, you can use adhesive dots to affix the square to the card. This will give it depth, another favorite Victorian look.

- Add lace with two-sided tape.

W Weavings

WOVEN PAPER STRIPS
average complexity

You can weave strips of paper and adhere them to the front of the card. The card shown is made from music photocopied on four different colors of paper and cut into strips. We've used a sort of simple basket weave for the paper strips.

MATERIALS

cardstock base

music or another motif

photocopier

colored paper

craft knife, paper cutter, or scissors

deckle scissors

two-sided tape

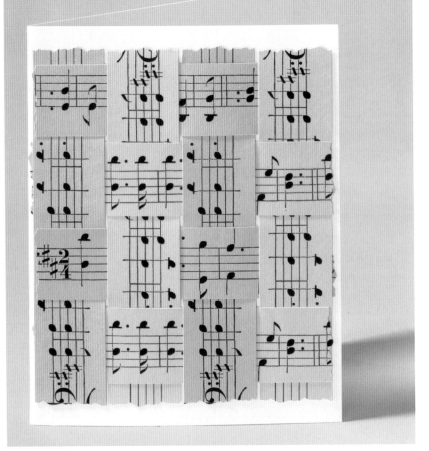

Use ready-made cardstock as a base.

Cut out the strips of music with a paper cutter, craft knife, or ordinary paper scissors. I've made my strips about 1 inch (2.54 cm) wide.

Trim the ends of the strips with deckle scissors to fit the front of the card.

Weave the strips over and under each other. Secure the strips underneath with two-sided tape to maintain the shape of the weave.

Adhere the woven strips to the cardstock with two-sided tape.

OTHER WEAVING OPTIONS

Use colorful fabric or other ribbons, raffia, or yarn instead of paper for weavings.

If you're a knitter, you could attach a woven cloth piece (scrap) on the card face. If you're really ambitious, it could be a mini-sweater, sock, or scarf with fringe. This would be a great gift card to include with a handmade knitted present, such as a full-size sweater. Satin ribbon would also be lovely.

Windows

feminine • scented

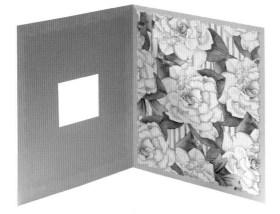

Pretty floral cards scented with a lovely fragrance are something a greeting-card e-mail cannot deliver. Just be sure that your recipient isn't allergic to perfumes, colognes, and other scents.

MATERIALS

cardstock base

spray bottle with perfume, cologne, or natural scent

2 coordinating decorative papers

craft knife

cutting mat

metal ruler

pencil

deckle scissors

glue stick

text (optional)

embellishments (optional)

- Begin with a cardstock base.

- With deckle scissors, cut a rectangle slightly smaller than the card face. Apply the glue stick to the whole underside of the decorative paper. Center the decorative paper on the card face and be sure that it is smooth and completely adheres to the cardstock.

- Open the card and lay it on a cutting mat with card front and back "covers" face up. With a ruler and a pencil, draw a small square in the desired size in the middle of the card's front cover where you want the window.

- With a craft knife, carefully cut away the window, using your ruler to make a clean cut. If you cut along the outside of your pencil line, the line will be gone when the cutaway square for the window is removed.

- Use deckle scissors to cut another decorative paper (we've chosen one with large flowers) for the inside (right-hand page) of the card. Apply glue with a glue stick to the back of the flowered decorative paper, center it on the right-hand page, and adhere it.

- Add a greeting to the front and inside of the card if you wish.

- When finished, spray just a little perfume or cologne on the back of the card.

Wire

quick and easy • masculine

Ready-made wire in various shapes and motifs can be found in arts and crafts stores. You can also buy thin wire to shape and create your own designs. Dress up the card with a few metallic-looking brads and you'll have a unique card. You can find a wire star, heart, or another symbol or figure that suits the receiver.

MATERIALS

cardstock

small fine wire object

star or other brads

wire thread

- Use a fairly firm ready-made cardstock or make your own.
- Punch a few holes with an ice pick or thin nail in the front of the card where you plan to fasten the wire motif. Be careful not to poke your fingers.
- Thread thin wire through the holes and fasten the small wire object (we've used a wire star) by wrapping the wire thread around the object.
- To finish the wire ends, twist them around a pencil to create the loop effect.
- Fasten the brads to the front of the card in a random layout.
- To hide your work and keep your receiver from being snagged on the brads, you could cover the inside of the "front cover" of the card with sturdy decorative paper, adhered with two-sided tape.
- Mail the finished card in a padded envelope.

Wood Texture

rustic • masculine • computer-aided design (optional)

For this card, I made a photo scan of wood texture and printed it out from my computer. (See handmade wood texture on p. 111.)

However, you don't need a computer to create wood texture. If the desired wood grain is "raised," you could make a rubbing on photocopy paper of the grain using a thick, flat crayon.

MATERIALS

photocopy or other paper

two-sided tape

clip art

computer

photo scanner

computer printout or handmade wood-grain paper

- Use a ready-made cardstock as your base.

- Cut out the wood-texture paper slightly smaller than the cover of your card cover. Add a border if you wish with your graphics computer program or a drawing pen and ruler.

- Adhere the wood-texture paper to the front of the card with two-sided tape.

- Cut out a clip art design and mount the clip art on top of the wood-grain paper. If you wish, you can add a border to the clip art.

Woolly Creature

quick and easy • fun • recycled

My dog decided to take apart my new sheepskin slippers. Since I found pieces of sheepskin all over the house, I gathered up the doggone pieces to make cards. If you don't have a pooch at home to do this prep work for you, polar fleece scraps will also work well. The wild eyes for this googly-eyed creature can be found in craft stores.

MATERIALS

cardstock

colored cardstock

scissors or paper cutter

black permanent marker

hard-bonding glue

googly eyes

polar fleece or sheepskin

sewing scissors

- Cut a piece of colored cardstock slightly smaller than the cardstock base to fit the front of the card. Adhere the colored cardstock to the cardstock base.

- With sewing scissors, cut an oval shape out of sheepskin or polar fleece.

- Using hard-bonding glue, mount the fleece to the card.

- With a black permanent marker, draw legs and a head so that the fleecy oval appears lamblike.

- Affix the googly eyes to the face with a dab of hard-bonding glue.

- Mail the card in a padded envelope.

X O X O

average complexity • computer-aided

Everyone knows that X O X O means kisses and hugs. Signal your love with this card. You can use multiple X's and O's in any way that suits you.

MATERIALS

cardstock base

decorative papers

computer or typewriter

photocopier (optional)

deckle scissors

two-sided tape or glue stick

decorative die-cut decal

- Cover an entire cardstock base with X O X O decorative paper using two-sided tape. If you cannot find X O X O paper, you can make it on your computer or even with an old-fashioned typewriter. Type or print on colored paper if you wish.

- With deckle scissors, cut a square or rectangle with a heart motif and adhere it to the card with two-sided tape.

- With solid paper and deckle scissors, cut out a heart slightly larger than the die-cut decal. Adhere the heart to the card. Affix the heart-shaped or other die-cut decal to the solid heart.

- Depending on the thickness of the die-cut decal, you may need to mail this in a padded envelope.

VARIATIONS: An option would be to photocopy a strip of X O X O's and paste or tape the multiple strips to a sheet of paper, and then photocopy the finished image on colored paper.

Or cut letters out of decorative paper and adhere them to decorative paper on the face of the card.

You could also make your own X's and O's with pen and ink on colored or plain paper, using fancy calligraphy. White out any imperfections and photocopy the results on colored paper. Be sure to clean the photocopier glass.

Yarn

average complexity • recycled

With so many fancy new yarns available today, you'll have fun choosing just the right one(s) to embellish your card. Or find a snippet of leftover yarn from a knitting project. You'll need less than 10 inches (25 cm), depending on your design. The corrugated cardstock was recycled from shipping packaging.

MATERIALS

firm cardstock base

stiff solid-colored paper

decorative papers

deckle scissors

scissors

corrugated card stock or recycled shipping packing

yarn

two-sided tape

one-sided tape

hard-bonding glue

craft knife

- Use a firm cardstock base.

- With deckle scissors, cut out a rectangle or square from stiff solid-colored paper. Adhere it to the cardstock base with two-sided tape.

- With deckle scissors, cut out a star shape from decorative paper. Adhere the star to the card with two-sided tape.

- With a craft knife, cut from corrugated stock a star shape that's a little smaller than your original decorative-paper star.

- Wrap a length of yarn around the star.

- Trim the two ends of yarn and secure them to the underside of the star with one-sided tape.

- Mount the star and yarn to the card with hard-bonding glue and let dry.

- Mail the finished card in a padded envelope.

HINT: Save items, like corrugated paper, that can be recycled into cards.

Yarn Magnets

average complexity • gift

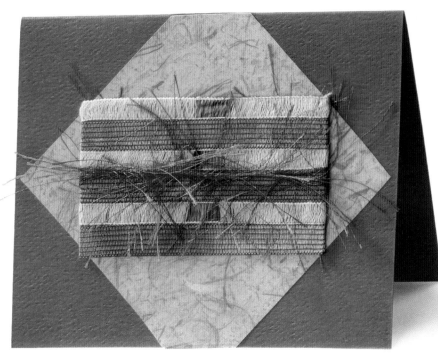

This card bears a magnet wrapped with decorative yarns. Some of the yarns we've used appear threadlike. Flexible magnets about the size of business cards are sold in packages found in office supply stores.

MATERIALS

cardstock

adhesive flexible magnet

decorative paper

yarn

scissors

deckle scissors (optional)

two-sided tape

- Begin with a firm cardstock base.

- From the decorative paper, cut a square, using deckle scissors if you wish. Adhere the square with two-sided tape in a diamond position to the cardstock base.

- Remove the protective paper from a flexible magnet.

- Cut lengths of different yarns and affix them to the sticky side of the magnet.

- Trim the excess yarn, allowing a little loose, fringy appearance if you wish.

- Position the magnet with its yarn where desired on the diamond. Fasten the magnet to the card with two-sided tape.

- Mail the finished card in a padded envelope.

Zigzags

average complexity • fun

All three examples of zigzag cards are created pretty much the same way. Photos and decorative paper can be used as part of a theme or just for fun.

MATERIALS

cardstock base

decorative paper

photo (optional)

craft knife

two-sided tape or glue stick

scissors

deckle scissors (optional)

hole punch (optional)

embellishments, such as gossamer ribbon (optional)

- Begin with the cardstock base.

- If you wish, first add a layer of decorative paper, cut with deckle scissors.

- Cut strips of decorative paper with deckle scissors, a craft knife, or ordinary scissors. They can be cut zigzag fashion or simply cut into strips and then arranged into a zigzag pattern.

- If you use a photo for your zigzag pattern, it's best to make your slices with a craft knife.

- Create a zigzag layout. Check the three finished cards shown here for ideas.

- Adhere the strips to the card using two-sided tape or a glue stick.

- Embellish as desired. We've used a gossamer ribbon threaded through a punched hole to enhance the photo zigzag card.

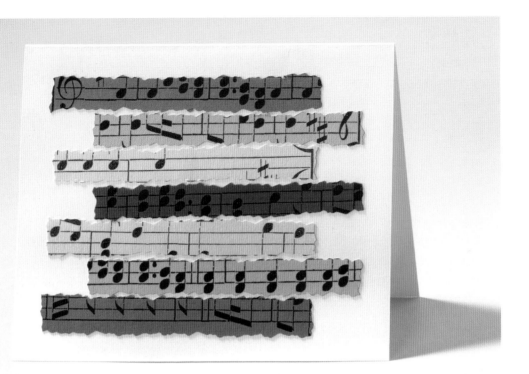

Acknowledgments

I would like to thank my editor, Jeanette Green, for her support and vision with this project. Hats off to the librarians at Cazenovia Public Library; they were key in assisting my research. I am deeply grateful to my dear husband Norman for understanding my need to meet deadlines and for forgiving dust bunnies and my time away from him. For all the pets featured in this book, I thank June for Pokie the cat, Maria for Sophia the Cavalier dog and that perfect peacock feather from her bird, and Barbara for Jazz and Tristan. Woof-woof! My special friends Sherie and Harry appear in some card photos. Avis and Luanne donated fabric scraps for a few projects. Other miscellaneous items came from local Cazenovia shops, garage sales, and friends. We've tried our best to locate the copyright owners of all materials used here.

We gratefully acknowledge the manufacturers, stores, and other companies that have provided their fine products and materials featured on various cards in this book. Note that the given company Web sites listed here were accurate at publication and are intended for product information only and not for sales or ordering products. Kindly check your local retailers for products.

Holiday cards from ©LPG Greetings, Inc., all rights reserved; Downeast Concepts, Inc., for the Beached Boat N-0302; the photo postcard of the city of Syracuse, New York, courtesy Anthony Mario of Margo Studio, Rome, New York; Paper Pizazz® and Cardmaker's™ patterned papers and foils are used with permission from Hot Off the Press, Canby, Oregon, www.paperwishes.com; Foamies™ and metal star ornament by Darice®; brads and decals from Joann™ Stores, Inc.; Paper Bliss™ tags by Westrim Crafts® and Collage Backgrounds™ papers by DMD, Inc.®; decals, stickers, and yarn from EK Success www.eksuccess.com; cards, tags, and stickers courtesy of Paper Magic Group; a special thank you to Colorbök for many donations of time and wonderful numerous supplies of paper, decals, mesh, stickers, yarn, brads, and more, www.colorbok.com; clip art from Dover Publications, Inc., www.doverpublications.com; decorative papers, quill decals, and stickers from Provo Craft, Inc., www.provocraft.com; ©C-Thru Ruler Company, Wonderful Words, www.cthruruler.com; decals from ©2004 me & my big ideas, Inc., all rights reserved under license; greeting card frames used with permission of Kristin Elliott, Inc.; embossed photo frames from Making Memories, www.makingmemories.com; photo magnets and stickers from Paper House Productions; Creative Hands® foam shapes #1621, Bug Love, www.creativehands.com; embossed photo frames from ©Masterpiece Studios, www.masterpiecestudios.com; Victorian stickers from Violette Stickers, www.violettestickers.com.; for Paper Shapers® shamrock punch by EK Success; LCI Paper Co, Inc., www.lcipaper.com; for scissors and tools by © 2005 PVA; Fiskars Brands, Inc., Fiskars.com; for die-cuts by Die Cuts with a View, 801-224-6766, www.diecutswithaview.com (wholesale information only); for lace doilies by Artifacts, Inc., www.Artifactsinc.com, 800-678-4178; and clip art from www.clipart.com.